BARE FEET
AND
TACKETY BOOTS

Archie Cameron

BARE FEET
AND
TACKETY BOOTS

A boyhood on Rhum

Archie Cameron

Luath Press Ltd.
Edinburgh

First Edition 1988,
Reprinted 1988
Reprinted 1990 (twice)
Reprinted 1992
Reprinted 1994
Reprinted 1997

The paper used in this book is produced from renewable forests and is chlorine-free.

Printed and bound by Gwasg Dinefwr Press Ltd., Llandybie

This book is dedicated to my family, and most especially to my mother and father. I can appreciate now what they did, and how they had to struggle to do it.

This book is published with the assistance of the Highlands and Islands Development Board. The Publisher also wishes to thank the Nature Conservancy Council for their very willing help.

Cover Picture:
Archie as a wee lad, or lass.

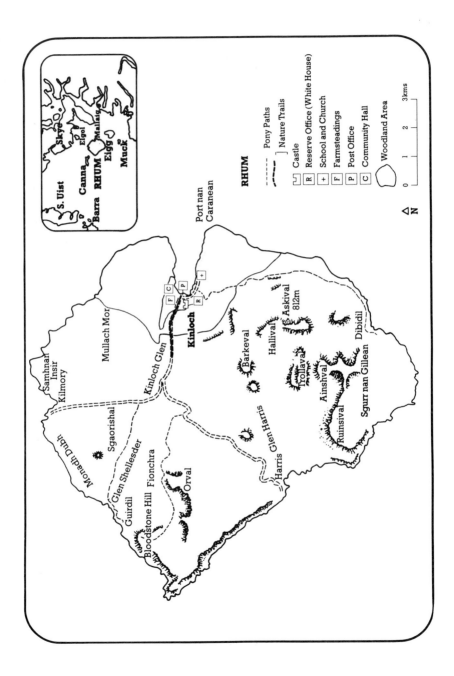

RHUM

- - - - - Pony Paths
――― Nature Trails

- ☐ Castle
- R Reserve Office (White House)
- + School and Church
- F Farmsteadings
- P Post Office
- C Community Hall
- ◯ Woodland Area

N

0   1   2   3kms

S. Uist
Canna RHUM
Barra Eigg
Skye Elgol Mallaig
Eigg Muck

Samhnan
Insir
Kilmory

Mullach Mor

Monadh Dubh

Sgaorishal

Glen Shellesder

Guirdil

Bloodstone Hill Fionchra

Orval

Kinloch Glen

Kinloch

F C
P
R +

Port nan
Caranean

Barkeval

Hallival

Askival
812m

Trollaval

Ainshval

Ruinsival

Sgurr nan Gillean

Dibidil

Harris Glen Harris

CONTENTS

INTRODUCTION.

The island of Rhum is in the Inner Hebrides, lying eight miles south of Skye and fifteen miles west of Mallaig in Morar.

Its present owners, the Nature Conservancy Council, and the Ordnance Survey, have settled on the name *Rhum*, although it could equally well be *Rum* — pronounced 'Room'. There is little philological justification for 'Rhum', since neither Gaelic nor Norse has an initial '*Rh*' sound, and it was Norse and Gaelic which gave names to all the features of the island.

It is an ancient name, with half a dozen fanciful theories about its origin. It perhaps originated in the Old Norse 'Romoy', although the island was also mentioned in the ancient Irish Annals of Tigernach. They tell of how St. Beccan lived there as a hermit, and died on the island about 676 A.D.

Not that he was by any means the first to live on Rhum. Indeed, the oldest remains of man in Scotland have been found at Kinloch, near where the castle now stands. These were Mesolithic people of 8,500 years ago. On the same site there are also remains of Neolithic people who lived there 4,000 years ago. Nearby are the remains of Iron Age occupation of 2,000 years ago. It should not be assumed, though, that there was continuous human occupation of the island over all those centuries. There may have been, but the historical record is still far from complete.

Quite certainly the Vikings knew Rhum well. Perhaps they gave the island its modern name, and without doubt they were responsible for many of the place names, especially the hills — Hallival (2,365 ft.), Ashival (2,659 feet — the highest on the island), Trallval, Ainshval, Rainsival — all are Norse names, and those hills were perhaps named because they are prominent and acted as landmarks for the sea-going Vikings.

From other place names, it also seems likely that there was some kind of early Christian settlement, although its site, if it exists, remains to be discovered. 'Kilmory' is the Church of Mary, and 'Papadil' the Dale of Priests. An ancient cross carved on a stone pillar has been found at Kilmory, and very possibly much still remains to be discovered.

Rhum is one of the larger of the Inner Hebrides, but it is nevertheless quite a small island, small enough to be well explored by the visitor in a few days. Roughly diamond shaped, it covers 26,400 acres, and is about eight and a half miles north to south and eight miles east to west. It is a rough little island, rockbound, with steep hills and narrow glens, and little in the way of arable land. Yet everywhere you turn there are remains of old deserted human habitations. Even high on the hills where there are some rich grasslands fertilised by the many thousands of Manx shearwaters that breed there, there are many remains of old shielings, the hovels where women and children spent the summer months, grazing their flocks, making butter and cheese for winter consumption, while the men remained below in the villages, tilling the land and perhaps fishing. There was a reliable census in 1795, and it was found that there were 443 inhabitants on the island then.

In 1824, a visitor recorded his impression that Rhum was '....*The wildest and most repulsive of the islands....If it is not always bad weather in Rum, it cannot be said to be good very often.*'

That was a rather strange reaction for its time, because it came when the wilder parts of England, Scotland and Wales were being 'discovered' for the first time. Better communications allowed easier travel, and the strange romanticism that fired such poets as Wordsworth was in full swing. It became fashionable to visit the wild places and to write travellers' tales of adventures, illustrated with engravings depicting a remoteness and savageness more suited to distant Tibet than, say, Scotland.

And yet, while assuredly it was a precarious, hand-to-mouth existence for the people in such places as Rhum, it certainly cannot have been all bad, either in economic or social terms.

The available land was organised by those who worked it on the ancient 'runrig' system, where every plot was re-allocated each year, so that no family consistently had bad or hard ground, and each had a turn at the good. The old, the weak, the widows and the sick all had their shares of land, which was worked for those unable to do it themselves. There were common grazings, with each family allocated a *'souming'* or proportion of the stock allowed on the land. There was mutual aid in the hard and endless work.

Cattle were reared, and sheep — the hardy native black cattle and the equally hardy small native sheep. Oats, bere barley and potatoes were grown on the strangely-named 'lazybeds'. (The people of Rhum, Gaelic speakers of course, would have called them *feannagan.*) The ridges of these can still be traced in a myriad places on the island. The fertiliser was seaweed, hard-won from the shores, and carried to the fields, usually by the women, using creels carried on their backs, supported by a strap round the forehead. Another fertiliser was the old soot-impregnated thatch from the cottages.

There were deer on the hills, of course, and you can still see traces of great walls leading to enclosures where the deer were driven and killed. There are the remains of at least one tidal fish trap, and as the author relates in this book, the seas were full of fish before the recent destruction of the breeding and feeding grounds by trawling.

The Manx shearwater, nesting in its many thousands on the hill tops, was yet another source of good eating, but rather oily, it was reported by a visitor. Those birds, which apart from their short breeding season, spend all their lives at sea, thousands of miles away off the coast of Brazil, were a year-long staple on many islands, salted and dried for the winter months.

Certainly it was a hard life, although, after centuries of clan warfare, when life was cheap, and at the mercy of unscrupulous clan chiefs and pretenders, it had settled to a rhythm that was precious enough. Indeed, with its highly developed system of mutual aid and care for the old and weak, there are lessons to be drawn for today.

Certainly, of course, it was not a bucolic idyll.   Life was harsh and work endless; it had always been so for those at the bottom of the economic pyramid.   Nevertheless, it was stable and secure, without the concentrated horror of the burgeoning industrial cities.

Idyllic or not, it produced little profit for McLean of Coll, whose claim to 'own' the island gave him supreme power over the lives of the islanders.   Like so many others, he had been suborned from his loyalty to his clan and to those who looked to him for support.   Like so many others, he had been 'bought by English gold', and joined the parcel of rogues who sold their kinsmens' birthright for the only thing those kinsmen could not give him — money.

Imbued with the highest form of Victorian morality — greed and profit — McLean leased the island to a relative, Dr. Lachlan McLean of Gallanach, and promptly all the islanders were given notice to quit their holdings and houses, and leave the island.   They were to leave by Whitsun, 1825, and they did.

Factor Alexander Hunter organised the Clearance.   On July 11th, 1826, three hundred people, young, old, men, women and children, were packed into vessels, ironically called the *Dove of Harmony* and the *Highland Lad*, and transported to Nova Scotia. There they were landed at Port Hawkesbury, to face the rigours and terrors of a harsh life in a new world, bereft of all that was dear and familiar, with their old society of co-operation and mutual aid shattered.

Even the Factor admitted that many 'were not willing to leave the land of their ancestors.'   In his booklet on Rhum, John A. Love quotes a shepherd, John McMaister, who witnessed the embarkation. *'He recalled the scene to be of such a distressful description that he would never be able to forget it to his dying day.   The wild cries of the men and the heart-breaking wails of the women and children filled all the air between the mountainous shores.'*

The good Dr. Lachlan McLean then found he had no-one to act as shepherds for his 8,000 sheep, so a dozen families being cleared off Mull and Skye were diverted to Rhum, to tend the thousands of sheep

4

which were scouring the island, destroying the ancient balance of growth and fertility.

It did not last long: the price of mutton collapsed: the sheep farming collapsed. The island became deserted, at least by humans. Nor did Dr. McLean flourish. He ended his days as an alcoholic medicine man in Oban. Even the house he built on the island, the Lodge, was cleared away when the Castle was built.

After him came the first English owner, no less a person than the 2nd. Marquis of Salisbury. He paid £26,455 for the island in 1845. For him, as for so many others, the Highlands and Islands represented mainly a vast sporting estate, to be used for fishing and hunting the deer. He organised the re-stocking of the island with red deer, and embarked on a considerable plan for development, with much drainage and building. He even had a dam built to improve the Kinloch river for fishing, but two days after its completion, the dam burst, to the considerable astonishment of the three hundred workers who had just finished their labours. Like so many other civil engineering works in the Highlands and Islands, this was done during the Potato Famine, when the wages of a hard day's labour was a handful of oatmeal. It was not considered proper to distribute charity: the indigent had to work for the little they needed to keep them alive, and if the work was done for the benefit of those kind enough to provide the oatmeal, well, that was only to be expected. And when there was no more work to be done, there was always the emigrant ship available. The Marquis 'gave assistance' for fifty-two people to leave for Canada in 1852.

Both the 2nd Marquis and his son, later Prime Minister, greatly increased the sheep stock on Rhum, and the count went up to approximately 10,000. The human population rose accordingly, of course, and in 1881 about ninety people lived permanently on the island.

By that time the Salisbury's had sold the island to a Mr. Campbell, but his ownership was brief, and in 1886 it passed into the hands of Mr. John Bullough, who paid £150,000 for it.

Bullough was wealthy, a self-made Lancashire man whose wealth — and it was very considerable — had come from various inventions and improvements in the textile trade. He is a rather misty figure, but one that would well repay study. Like so many others of his time and background, he had become enamoured of the Highlands and Islands, and of the sporting facilities there. He had rented the shooting on Rhum for several years before purchasing the island.

John Bullough did not live long to enjoy his new possession, but he did begin sweepimg changes and developments. Shooting lodges were built, extensive tree planting done and the deer stock refreshed with stags imported from England. Rhum was not his only Scottish estate; he also had a considerable spread in Perthshire, but for some reason he chose to be buried on Rhum. However, his infatuation with the place did not seem to extend to the people, and he allowed only three families to remain on Rhum when he became proprietor. The rest he sent away and replaced them with others.

John Bullough died in 1891, and George Bullough, later Sir George, inherited the island. George was on a world tour when his father died, having been sent away, rumour had it, because of a too-close relationship with his young step-mother. Kinloch Castle today contains many souvenirs of George Bullough's world tour, and of his subsequent travels.

Sir George had ideas more grandiose than those of his dead father. He was not content with the Lodge built by Dr. Lachlan McLean, and embarked on building Kinloch Castle, a vast, ostentatious edifice of red Arran sandstone, whose very colour, let alone its design, is totally foreign to its island environment.

Those were strange days in the Highlands. Enormous estates had been taken over by those newly enriched in the great mid-Victorian burgeoning of industry and trade. They were not interested in the land as a source of produce or even profit. It was their plaything, a place to be visited for shooting and fishing, and, for a few weeks each year, to act out their dreams of lairdship and Highland life. Although rapidly attaining political power in the country, they, in their generation anyway, could never hope to be accepted socially in what they enviously saw as the highest circles. Even when their efforts and money led them to be en-nobled, they were still 'trade', and never quite made it into the top layer of society.

On their vast estates, they reigned supreme. There, they were the topmost of the top. They need mix only with their own kind, and their own guests, and the owners of other estates, and *their* guests, mostly people of their own kind.

It was not enough to have a vast, empty estate, peopled only by gamekeepers, stalkers and a few shepherds. They demanded enormous castles, like Kinloch and the equally preposterous Glenborrodale in nearby Ardnamurchan, in which they played out their dreams. They demanded great steam yachts in which they travelled the lochs of the Highlands — and indeed travelled the world. Those yachts were big enough to play a more sombre role as hospital ships when that dream-world collapsed in 1914.

Jesse Boot the Cash Chemist, Clark of Clark's Thread, Sir George Bullough, and many more of immense wealth, owned great estates as their playgrounds and played their childish games on lands once productive and well-populated, but then reduced to the emptiness of deer forests, peopled only by those employed to cater to the whims of their masters.

In this book, Archie Cameron tells of life on Rhum from the worm's eye view, and it is a fascinating story, especially when contrasted with the unthinking display of seemingly untold wealth by the proprietor. With the innate kindliness and respect of the Highlander, he has little to say of the gentry, but his scorn and contempt for Factors is unbounded. Of course, the Factor, as the chief agent of the proprietor, was a man of great power, but that power was delegated to him, and the ultimate responsibility lay with the proprietor for all good and evil done by his servant. Right throughout the terrible times of the Clearances and through the seeming tranquillity of life on the great estates, it was the Factor who gave the orders, and only too often it was the Factor himself who put the torch to the cottages. But he acted always as the agent for the proprietor, and under his — or her — orders.

Archie Cameron makes Sir George Bullough appear to be a kindly enough man, and fairly innocuous. Lady Monica, the French wife of Sir George, also seems to have been kindly enough, and certainly Archie had a deep affection for her. But it is other characters who really live in these pages, and especially perhaps Archie's own father, a sterling figure whom one would have loved to know.

The estate never recovered its former glories after the war of 1914-18. Not only was money more scarce, but somehow the very spirit of the great estates seemed to have been buried, with so much else, in Flanders mud. There was no more development; the gardens and policies were put on a care-and-maintenance basis, and altogether the life of the pre-war years never reappeared. However, Sir George continued to visit the island and his castle right up to his death in 1939. Lady Monica was rarely there after that, and in 1957 she sold the island to the Nature Conservancy Council. She herself lived on for twelve years, to die at the grand age of ninety-eight. John Bullough, Sir George and Lady Monica are all buried on Rhum, in a totally fantastic mausoleum on the west coast of the island at Harris. Until the mausoleum was built, John Bullough was buried in a cave hewn from the rock nearby.

For many years, from 1843 to 1957, when it was a private estate, Rhum had the reputation of being a 'closed island', and indeed visitors, except their own guests, were never welcomed by the proprietors. Now it is owned by the nation, and run, extremely efficiently, by the Nature Conservancy Council.

As an island, Rhum is the ideal testing ground for many experiments in conserving and restoring the natural life of the Highlands. Furthermore, although not attempting to preserve simply for the sake of preserving, the Council is now able to give permanent protection to the very many features of scientific interest on the island. It preserves the habitat of the wildlife; it seeks to restore the native woodland and increase the various plant and animal communities.

Although so comparatively small, Rhum is a very precious microcosm of the Hebrides, packed with interest and beauty. There are vast cliffs tumbling sheer to the sea, harsh and rugged hills, narrow glens loud with swift burns, astonishing green hill tops fertilised by many generations of countless Manx shearwaters. There are deer, carefully controlled and studied, wild ponies, wild goats, otters and seals.

It is no part of this book to describe the work of the Nature Conservancy Council on Rhum. They do that themselves, very efficiently and readably, in their own publications. But what they have done is open up the island to discerning visitors, who can stay in that staggering Edwardian castle, surrounded by the opulence of a by-gone age, and relive for a few days the life of a Highland proprietor of eighty years ago.

The island is small enough to be well explored on foot — there is no alternative! The great kitchen gardens and greenhouses, the rose garden, the Italian garden, the orchards and turtle ponds have gone. (Home made turtle soup was held to be a great restorative after a hard day stalking the red deer.) The policies around the castle no longer have fourteen gardeners trimming and snipping at them. The sheep, too have gone, and so have the shepherds, those hardy men who walked the fells day by day.

But it is not the shepherds who haunt those hills and straths. Rather, it is those who made their lives on the island for centuries before the Great White Sheep appeared — those who, bewailing their fate, were packed into the holds of the *Dove of Harmony* and the *Highland Lad* and shipped to a strange and savage land.

TOM ATKINSON

9

PREFACE

My sister Mary believed she knew what a 'Preface' is. It was one of the first things she learned in the High School in Oban. She brought her new knowledge home to us, of course, and the first spark of erudition was kindled in our young and receptive minds when she told us that the letters of the word, forward and backward, represented the jingle *Peter Robertson eating fish Andrew catching eels: eels catching Andrew's feet eating rotten plums.*

How's that for High School education? But it wasn't all that kind of nonsense, and she went on to learn a lot of other things that were of more use to her, and she retired as a teacher in a college in Edinburgh.

I know that a 'Preface' is a sort of introduction or resume of what is to follow, and yet I never went to High School. I was never even asked if I wanted to go. It would have been a waste of time anyway: I was never consulted about my future or where I wanted to go. I was told where to go and there I went without any demur. I was never even asked if I wanted to be born, or where. That may have been fortunate, as, had I been consulted, I might easily have chosen a less salubrious place than Rhum in which to draw my first breath and make my first squawk. But things turned out all right without any decision by me. My parents chose the place and the approximate date, and that was the eighth day of April, Nineteen Hundred and Three. I am unable to state the time, but that is largely irrelevant. The date, on the other hand, I have grown up with, and have been asked to write it and state it in so many countries that I am not likely to forget it. The place — well, my parents made a good choice, and if asked, when I had reached a stage of maturity that gave me the ability to answer a sensible question in an intelligent manner, I would have applauded their decision to have me born on the Island of Rhum.

Some of my unborn brothers and sisters were carried away by my mother, to be born in such outlandish places as Tolsta, in Lewis, and Oban, making them, literally, incomers to Rhum, where we made our home.

I was the third child, but the first son. My father doted on me, and consequently I was a very spoiled and impudent wee brat. The first two girls were Mary and Dinah, and after me came Joey, Iain, Donnie and Dougie. My mother was thirty-two when she married, and she had laid the foundations of a dynasty before Nature called '*Enough!*

Certainly, living on that delectable island until I had reached the age of about sixteen ensured that when the time came to leave (and that was not my choice) I was a complete neophyte in all matters pertaining to earning my living and making my way in entirely new, albeit most interesting, surroundings. I began serving my time as a gardener in the extensive gardens on the island, and I followed that occupation for some years after I left Rhum. I was then a very raw youngster, but I learned fast, and ultimately arrived, almost unscathed, at where I am today. But that's another story which I am ready and willing to relate to anyone who is sufficiently interested to request it.

There was a permanent outdoor staff of between forty-five and fifty on the island, and as many as twenty-four children in the school. At the height of the 'season' of course, the island population was increased by the castle staff of about thirty, and that did not include the crew of the yacht *Rhouma*. They lived on the yacht, but made occasional forays ashore, chiefly to play football against one of our island teams. There were no less than three football teams on Rhum at that time.

We did not come into contact with the Gentry, and in fact were instructed by our parents to keep out of their way if we saw them approaching. When they did sometimes stumble across us, they were invariably kind and chatty. But Sir George himself, although on friendly enough terms with all the workers, and although addressing them by their given names, liked to act the austere Highland Laird.

The village in which we lived was Kinloch, and as the name implies (*Ceann Loch* — Head of the Loch), it was situated at the head of the loch. There were nine houses there, as well as the 'Yard', and the Farm Manager's house was at the Yard, together with the garages for the Albion cars, the chauffeurs' rooms, the byres and horse boxes and

12

such things as tack and harness rooms.

My father had a very interesting and satisfying forty-six years on the island, in the position of ghillie, boatman, alligator and turtle keeper, with a little surreptitious poaching on the side.

In the 'off-season', my father and Angus Thwaite, another ghillie, spent most of their time repairing roads. Due to the heavy rainfall, this was a constant job, and at times they would be stationed at Harris, coming home only for the weekend. That area, with its many steep gradients, was very susceptible to washouts, and the roads had to be made up with broken stone which was 'knapped' by the two men. It must have been very hard work, but I think they had some fun too. On one occasion I overheard my father telling my mother that they had chased and killed a sheep and had eaten their way through it during their week's exile. When they were not actually eating bits of it, the carcase was kept under the mattress of a spare bed, in case the factor made a surprise visit!

We seven children had a very happy home life, particularly in the evenings when my father was at home and organising us in various forms of entertainment. On wet days, when we were unable to get outside, and were at loose and obstreperous ends, my mother would sometimes haul out of the cupboard a large earthenware jar and pour onto the floor a big dollop of mercury! Where it had come from and why she had it I never did learn until years later, but we children spent many happy hours chasing it about the floor until the dollop eventually disappeared into the cracks of the linoleum.

It was fun, and it kept us amused, but I know now that it was very dangerous stuff, and I suppose that the quick-silver, as we called it, still rests somewhere in the foundations of the old house, waiting perhaps to confuse some metal-detecting enthusiast in the future.

I believe it was very valuable stuff, and was left in our house by a lodger who was one of the electricians installing the electrical system and water turbine for the island (which was claimed to be big enough to provide electricity for the whole of Glasgow). Be that as it may, we were quite happy to have the mercury to play with.

13

My sister Dinah, however, being less adventurous than the rest of us, contented herself by playing with a clock that had been given to her by Bella, one of the maids who worked in the castle. While we were busy poisoning ourselves, she would slip away, and, drawing her mother's attention by pulling at her skirt, would lisp 'Mamma, di mee wee cockie cattle Belly bing cattle peal.' My mother was able to translate this into 'Mamma, give me the wee clock that Bella brought from the castle, please.'

I cherish many happy memories of life on Rhum, both indoors and out. The annual staff picnic to Kilmory, for example in the shining Albions, always seemed to take place on sunny days. Two horse-drawn carts went ahead, laden with the necessary food produced by the castle kitchens and carrying all the spare produce of the Castle gardens and greenhouses — grapes, nectarines, peaches, green figs and strawberries, I remember — all the exotic things of which we had hardly heard before, and certainly never tasted. It was always an ambition of we lads to find a safe way into those gardens and raid them, but we never did it, for it had been well impressed on us that they were totally Forbidden Territory, and any transgression of that law meant instant banishment from the island for the transgressor and his whole family. It was about the only Commandment (and there were many) we dare not break.

Anyway, on that one day of the year we were able to eat our fill. We were loaded into the gleaming Albions and carried away in real Gentry style over the miles to Kilmory, miles that we often trudged but rarely rode. I still remember the smell of the exhaust from those Albion engines. It seemed very fragrant, and far removed from the stink of petrol today.

It was a treasured day out for us, and must have been a welcome interlude in the lives of the two sequestered laundry maids there, who spent the whole season of about three months tucked away at Kilmory, five miles from the village. It would never do to have the laird, his lady and their aristocratic guests looking out of the castle windows to find the area polluted with shirts and dainty underwear!

The laundry, like so much else, is now a ruin, and no more do the silk shirts wave across the sea to the inhabitants of Canna.

Gone, too, is the large pack of 'Black and Tan' game dogs: the superb, but now empty kennels no longer resound to their barking in the summer mornings.

Silenced, too, is the boat, the brainchild of Eric Cottrel, one of the chauffeurs, which tore up and down the loch, driven by an aerial propellor. Did Eric go on to bigger things? I have always regretted that I have never found out, for Eric was one of those who did not come back after the break-up of the establishment.

There is now very little left but pleasant and intriguing memories, for me and a few more who still stagger around. Fortunately, we still have these memories: they cannot decay or moulder, but are enhanced and magnified by the passing of the years.

When the island of Rhum hummed with life and activity, it was a wonderful and exciting place in which to spend one's childhood. There was, however, a somewhat un-nerving experience which we encountered almost every day on our way to school. The school opening time seemed to coincide with the pack of game dogs being taken out for their usual morning run. 'Dina' the friendliest dog in the pack, had the terrifying method of showing her affection by rushing up with her fangs bared in a huge smile. This approach we neither appreciated nor understood, and I can still hear the crack of Donald's whip and his cries of 'Dina!, Dina!'. Despite the fact that we gradually overcame our fear of the animals, it was always with feelings of relief that we waded through the last of the pack, some of them big beasts, and it *was* a bit alarming to have a flapping tongue and big sharp teeth stuck in your face.

That was one trial overcome, but there was much worse to follow.

Peter Jopp, our alcoholic teacher's devilish face, was also grinning and showing its fangs, but it was not smiling like Dina.

His stealthy approach, with finger crooked, and the snarl of 'Come in aboot' boded no good for the one who was called out. The very soul was chilled with terror.

Although some of our teachers were Gaelic speakers, our native language was not used in school. There were only about six of us whose mother tongue was Gaelic: the rest were children of workers from non-Gaelic areas of the mainland, and even from England. Consequently, we were taught in English, and then never even thought it strange or wrong that we were compelled to grow up as English-speaking children. Fortunately, though, a lot of our singing was done in the Old Language. I believe our teachers knew more Gaelic songs than English ones!

Thankfully, though, the school day ended with our escape at four o'clock, but we were not always unscathed. There would be bruises, abrasions and torn clothing to explain away when we got home, but not how they had been acquired. We would have got no sympathy anyway, and the damage and injuries done by a sadistic teacher were passed off as rough play.

Our favourite playground was the shore, where there were so many things to do that would make us forget our recent harrowing experiences. We improvised boats and rafts from driftwood and when they were available, fashioned little boats from the leaves of the bog iris. Those wee boats were the fastest things on water that I have ever seen, and with a favourable wind would leap from the crests of the wavelets and disappear in the distance in a few minutes.

We had many diversions in this area, such as launching Neill in an iron bath, with one paddle to propel and navigate his recalcitrant craft. It was not a success, and after a few giddy whirls the bath went over. There were no volunteers for a retrial.

We would occasionally leave the shore and make for the high ground, where we would spend the day rolling boulders from the tops, with highly satisfactory and thrilling results as they bounced and crashed down to the sea, leaving a trail of sparks and splinters.

Our day on the hill was quite as thrilling as that of the gentry, and a lot cheaper. We also carried home our own array of trophies in the shape of a collection of heather ticks. When we got home we would pick these off, with the exception of one outstanding specimen.

This selected beastie had to be in a position where it could be shown on request or demand. The wee beastie was nurtured with loving care. It was undemonstrative, and not as amusing or entertaining as a cat or dog, but we had neither of those: the wee tick was ours and we lavished our affection on it, and it was less demanding than a bigger and livelier pet would have been. All he wanted to do was to be left alone, hanging on to his oasis, his face buried in the never-ending supply of nutrition, which was not grudged him. The surrounding area of the oasis got very itchy, and would be scratched carefully, to avoid alarming the wee thing. Each morning we would ask after the wellbeing of the other ticks, and proudly display our own. This would go on for about a week, until one morning there would be only a red blotch where our pet had been. We were then able to give the whole area a good scratching, and that was quite a relief, but we missed the wee beast when we looked at the vacant patch.

There was a mandatory ban on private cats and dogs, and it may be that, being deprived of the affection and pleasure those animals could have given us, we improvised and made the most of what was available.

We also made the best of our little school, into which was crowded twenty or more children, aged from five to fourteen, and all packed into one room, and if it did not produce any professors, most of us did quite well in our various pursuits. I myself have had a bit of a scrambled life, but an exciting and satisfying one. My sister Mary was a school teacher. My brother Donnie was awarded the M.B.E. while a driver in the Scotland Yard Flying Squad. Iain retired as Chief Inspector of Police, and my two remaining sisters reached eminent positions in their chosen careers of catering and hospital work.

FACTORS & HOME ENTERTAINMENT

Much has been written — and will be written — about the romanticised life of the gentry on the island of Rhum during the luxurious reign of Sir George and Lady Monica Bullough, a way of life which was, like so many other ways of life, brought to a sad end with the outbreak of the Great War in 1914. If there are any unanswered questions regarding life on the island at that time, I believe I am one of the very few still living able and willing to answer them.

The life of the gentry has been well explored and much written about, but there were also those who made the whole machine work, and it is the life of those, the 'serfs', with which I am concerned.

During the Season, when everything revolved round the Castle and its occupants, nobody had much time or inclination for private pursuits, and indeed most of the island was out of bounds to the natives.

Out of the Season, which was only about three months each year, it was a different matter, and, apart from the policies immediately around the Castle, our freedom was almost unbounded.

There was, though, a worm in the apple. When the Laird and his gracious Lady had returned to their winter residence in the south, we were left to the merciless and villainous factor, and with no redress against his wicked decisions. The one I remember as the most virulent was, after many years of villainy, instantly dismissed on one occasion when Sir George returned to the island. That evil being was last heard of trying to sell books to his erstwhile friends in Mallaig. That particular tyrant, when Willie and I were earning ten shillings a week,'fined' us both £1 for taking one of the small boats to go fishing without his permission. Our parents felt this was fairly lenient, as, had we complained to Sir George, as I threatened to do, both families could have been expelled. As it was, my threat alone resulted in a month's notice for me, and I was thrown off the island. We later learned that all letters of complaint sent to Sir George were attended to by his secretary, who returned them to the factor for his comments. Sir George never saw them, and in Willie's case and mine, the factor made the final decision: dismissal without appeal.

One elderly shepherd of my acquaintance, who had plenty of experience of both, said that the curse of the Highlands was midges and factors, and the worst was the factor. I agree with the sentiment, and do not even like writing about the vermin. But I will have more to say about the least objectionable of them in a later chapter.

Our main winter activities were largely of our own making, and consisted mostly of draughts, when a few of the boys would gather in someone's house and compete against each other. Cards were very much frowned upon as being the 'Devil's Bible', and were not played in our house.

A large recreation hall had been built, but on completion was found to be useless on account of the acoustics, or lack of them. The reverberating echoes were almost unbelievable; if one shouted in that hall, it sounded like a hundred voices.

Electricity was not brought to the island until the hall had been completed, and the place had been built under candle light. Bales of those special green candles were strewn all over the place, and the rats, finding them a delicacy, carried them off in large numbers. When it was finished, the hall was fitted out with many indoor amusements, such as table tennis, billiards and badminton, but was very little used on account of the excessive noise. We were therefore compelled to revert to our own previous indoor entertainments at home.

Ours was not a large house, and certainly in the later years it was crowded.   The main centre of activity was the living room, where all domestic operations were carried out.   The huge coal-burning range was there, which roared like the stoke-hold of a destroyer when the wind was right, and seemed to burn almost as much coal.   The front door opened off the living room, straight into the garden which provided us with all our potatoes and vegetables.   I spent many hours in that garden, throwing stones to keep out the hens and their valiant leader, the big Rhode Island Red Cock.   The back door led into the back kitchen and scullery, which was floored with very cold concrete.

Upstairs was one big room, which contained four beds, three of them made by the master of the house, and all seven children slept there, huddling like a litter of pups and listening, in their respective season, to the gales, the corncrakes and the roaring of the stags.

Those houses were good for the summers, but draughty old places in the winters.   Gathered round the 'furnace' on a cold winter's night, we could watch the lino billowing like waves as the wind roared up through the cracks in the floorboards.   My mother would sit among the billows, knitting, perhaps, or sewing, or making rag mats, while my father cobbled our boots, with the big paraffin lamp pulled down on its chains to give him more light.   My parents' bedroom opened off the living room, and was just as draughty.   It was no place to sit and primp and make up, even had my mother even dreamed of such God-less activities.   Of course there was no bathroom in any of the cottages, and we were dipped and scrubbed in a tin bath in front of the range.   Our tin bath was special, and must have come from some level of society far above ours.   It was a luxury model, with a head rest and bulging arm rests.   We never had time to enjoy such luxuries, though, for there was always a queue waiting for both the bath and the bathwater.   As we grew up, we were upgraded, and chased out to the washhouse one at a time to slosh around in the water left in the boiler on washing days.

My father was very much a family man, and enjoyed arranging and supervising activities for his family of three girls and four boys.   He was a master exponent of Highland dancing, and would often start off

21

the evening with demonstrations of the Sword Dance, Highland Fling and other solo exhibitions. When his repertoire in that line was exhausted, he would snatch the sewing or knitting from my mother's hands, sweep her on to the floor and line her up with the rest of us to make up an Eightsome or Scotch Reel. He provided the 'mouth music' himself, whistling, panting and puffing while he danced and directed his conscripted pupils.

His joviality seemed to be more pronounced and energetic when he was short of tobacco, which was a frequent disaster, on account of the late arrival of the steamer. Bad weather often prevented her calling at Rhum, and it was a sad sight to see her sailing past with all our much-needed supplies (especially tobacco) being taken out to Barra, or maybe back to Oban. Anyway, if my father had a supply of tobacco, he would probably be sitting in his round cosy chair by the fire, puffing away in peace. As it was, the lack of the wherewithal to fill his pipe seemed to make him restless and appeared to put mettle in his heels as he spun around like a Dervish, no doubt in an effort to diminish his craving. The members of his diminutive team, together with my mother, would be whirled and birled in wild abandon, like leaves in a winter's gale until he collapsed panting and puffing into his armchair, fingers probing the pockets of his waistcoat in yet another vain search for a pipe 'dottle'. His team would drift away to their favourite corners, the wild, startled look slowly disappearing from their faces.

Apart from those home festivities we had communal dancing in the servants' hall in the castle. The fiddle music was provided by Neil McLean, nicknamed by us 'The Doudle', because he carried his music into his work as a joiner. When sawing or planing a piece of wood in his workshop he would keep time to the action with blasts of 'Hi The Doodilum The Do Do Di'. He was as good a fiddler as he was a joiner, and while pretending to be bad tempered and annoyed at our pleadings, would, with a few swipes of his plane, shape out a lovely wee boat, which our mothers fitted out with sails and which gave us many happy hours at the burn. Our rigging of some of those models seemed to be faulty, as occasionally one of them would only sail backwards. This, however, gave us no cause for lament: in fact it increased the ego of the owner of such a boat to be able to boast that his model could outsail the others while going backwards!

Neil McLean, our boatbuilder, joiner and fiddler, from his seat at the top of the hall, must have had a good chuckle at the uncouth mob tangling on the floor in front of him, prepared to leap and whirl in all directions to the sound of his fiddle. It was no mannequin parade, I assure you. Our most pressing problem was getting our hands on suitable footwear in which we would be able to dance. Some startling examples of footwear were invariably on display, and anyone wearing a proper pair of dancing shoes was considered to be putting on airs and rising out of his or her proper station in society.

Our main source of supply was the rag-bag into which all the discarded clothing and footwear was dumped to await the arrival of the Macallisters, the sea-tinkers who called periodically to collect the stuff. They also took stags' horns which we collected on the hills during the casting season, usually about April. Incidentally, I may mention that we made a good jelly from the stag horn. There was quite a 'staggy' flavour about it, but we did not object to that as we were fond of venison anyway, and we did not have much else in the way of sweetmeats to compare it with. I believe the horns taken away by the tinkers were also made into a jelly, but that was for industrial use and not for human consumption. Anyway, what we made did us no harm, and was very acceptable to us. In return for the horns and rubbish collected by the sea-tinkers, we were given 'Toby Jugs' and beautifully hand painted plates, some of which are still to be seen at the family 'headquarters' in Corpach, and which I believe are now quite valuable as collectors' pieces.

Well, that was the mother-lode in which we scrabbled for our dancing equipment. As our common and everyday footwear was tacketty boots, there was usually a frenzied scurrying around, a day or two before the dance, and all dumps of household debris carefully screened for any sort of discarded shoes.

I myself was fairly fortunate in unearthing a discarded pair of my sister's shoes, high heels and all, which, with a string around the instep, were a reasonable fit. It must have been very amusing for the adults who were granted this display of ancient models. We, of course, were quite oblivious to this, and were perfectly happy as we leaped around in our borrowed, begged or pinched improvisations.

Those Macallisters were interesting people. They did the same job as other tinkers, but their route took them to all the Small Isles, travelling in a single-masted boat of no more than thirty feet. Probably because they could not carry it, they were not interested in scrap metal, but almost everything else was welcome.

In Rhum, they were especially interested in the cast stag horns, which we children gleaned from the hills. Incidentally, one particular beast of a factor tried to rob me of my haul one day, stating he was entitled to charge me half-a-crown for the cast horns, because they were the property of Sir George. I dumped them, and then collected them up again after dark. Even as a small child it took a smart factor to put anything over on me! The tinkers emptied the rag-bag and every other source of what was to us useless rubbish, and then offered the housewife her choice of dishes from their basket.

The Macallisters were respectable people, and very respected — perhaps even envied a little. There was no special reason to lock up the poultry when they were on the island. Their scow was usually anchored in a sheltered bay in front of the school house, and their children, of which there were several, would come ashore where we made friends with them, until the teacher warned us to keep away because they were 'dirty'. That puzzled us, because they seemed no dirtier than we were, and we were normal and acceptable enough, even by the prim standards of some teachers. With several young children, two adults and at least one dog on a small boat, the standards of cleanliness could not be very high, anyway. We allowed for that, and accepted them, dirt and all. It was only several years later that I came to realise that the teachers' 'dirt' was not our normal dirt, but lice. It was much later still that, when crossing over to Luing one day, I was delighted to meet the skipper of the boat, and found it was one of the 'dirty' wee boys who had played with us on the shore on Rhum. The family had prospered greatly, and this man now owned his own cabin cruiser and was preparing for a tour of the islands he had travelled as a small boy. He kindly invited me to join him, but I had to decline, and content myself with wishing him a safe voyage, and go on my way, wishing that it could have been his way.

For entertainment between the dances in the winter evenings, it was about this time that I broke into the interesting sport of poaching. This was not in a very big way — yet — but being by now about eleven years old, I thought I was qualified to take my place as a provider of the family needs, in a modest way.

The potato field near the house was my 'trap line'. After the tubers had been lifted, there were usually some left in the ground, just below the surface. Large numbers of ducks came in at night to feed on them, and how the ducks found them in the dark puzzled me, but find them they did. I found them in the daylight, after the ducks had uncovered and eaten part of them.

A carefully placed rat trap near one of the poor duck's caches invariably produced a duck, caught by the leg. The very first one I caught had the quesiontable distinction of teaching me that a duck's neck cannot be pulled like a hen's!

Clasping my capture tightly to my bosom, I hightailed it for the henhouse, where I intended to complete the operation of turning a live duck into a dead one. I closed the henhouse door, held the duck by its webbed feet and pulled its neck. This was certainly effective: the head came away in my hand and the duck flew round in circles, a gruesome projection which should have carried its head spurting blood on the walls. I was horrified and shocked by this experience, but not sufficiently so to stop me trapping ducks.

As those birds, like deer, were considered Royal Game, we never referred to them as ducks. Someone might hear a carelessly spoken word and get a clue as to what we were up to. We called them *Casean Dearg*, which is Gaélic for Red Feet, and we considered this enough to put the uninitiated off the scent.   We had many good meals off the Red Feet.

When the duck season came to an end, I expanded my operations and branched out into trout.   Having gained confidence in this sport, I one day offered to take my sister for a walk.   She, in all innocence, was quite delighted to accompany me, and we made our way up the hill behind the castle, which was seething with Gentry at the time.

When we had reached a satisfactory stretch of burn, my sister's face became loud with horror as she watched me produce a small fishing rod from my trouser leg.   The hazard of imminent discovery only enhanced the pleasure of my sport, and as an Aberdonian friend of mine would say, I got some grand trooties.   My sister was not amused!

I sickened my father one day, though, with what I considered to be an outstanding catch.   Taking a leisurely stroll by the turbine pond one Sunday afternoon, without a predatory thought in my head, I saw a beautiful big sea trout cooried in against the wall of the dam.   This immediately put all thoughts of the Sabbath out of my mind, and I was ready for any sacrilege.   I hastened home, and, unobserved, dodged into the wash-house and fixed up a line with one big hook.   Back at the pond, I carefully lowered the hook until it was immediately under the trout's chin.   One quick jerk and a heave put the trout on the grass at my feet.   With commendable prudence, I concealed the fish.   My parents, being very religious and Sabbath-minded, looked on Sunday fishing as a sure way to eternal damnation.   Subterfuge was the only way out, and the trout was carefully hidden in the coolness of the shrubbery, where it lay until I retrieved it and brought it home, triumphantly, on Monday morning.

My father much enjoyed his share of the trout, but had barely stopped wiping his lips when my perfidy was revealed.   I do not remember how, but it was probably by one of my younger brothers or sisters who had not been given a portion of the fish, and did not realise the enormity of my offence.   It did not take my father as long to swallow this revelation as it had to swallow the trout, but when he had grasped what he had just been told, there were startling repercussions. His expression changed rapidly from relaxed repletion to that of horror.

He spluttered and raved for a good ten minutes, as the full culpability of his own sin in the eyes of The Lord became apparent. He tried to throw up the offending fish, but I have a sneaking feeling that his attempts were lacking in real effort or intent.

To say that my father was economical would be an understatement. He was almost as dedicated to that as he was to his religion, and I believe that in this instance economy won. There was no emission and therefore nothing was wasted, but an aura of gloom seemed to hang over him for the rest of the day.

There was no more said about the unhappy affair, but I have no doubt that other trout brought in by me were viewed with suspicion.

Fish and 'Red Feet' were by now becoming small fry, and as there was nothing else to go for but deer, I decided to have a go at them. I had no intention of chasing them over the moor, however, as my father had done. There was one rascal of a stag which made a habit of entering our garden through a narrow passage at the end of the house and eating our cabbages. I decided that this was where I would make my debut.

I fashioned a snare from very strong wire and fastened it to the end of the house. This was to be, I was sure, my first big kill, but I had not reckoned on the strength of a trapped stag. When I went out into the cold grey dawn, I was shaken to the soles of my tacketty boots when I saw all that was left of my snare — a small remnant, stuck out of the side of the house like a pencil, snapped clean, without a bend or a kink. This made me realise for the first time the incredible strength of those animals, and gave my enthusiasm for catching them a severe dent. It also made me think a lot more of my father's accomplishment in catching one on the open moor and holding it by the leg until he eventually brought it down and killed it.

Well, there it was: my first capture away, snare and all.

I smartly removed the evidence of my poaching attempt, as there was the danger of Donald, our gamekeeper neighbour, getting a look at it and, later, seeing a stag wearing a wire necklet, would metaphorically connect the two. The scheme was riddled with dangerous possibilities, and was abandoned. Nevertheless, my ambition to obtain a stag nibbled away for many a year. Later, after I had left the island and was employed on the mainland, I arrived home on my annual leave with a gun packed in my luggage. That did not get me a stag, either, nor, certainly, did it get me the approbation of my mother when the weapon was revealed to her. Indeed, that was the only time my departure was more welcome than my arrival.

Those setbacks, however, did not dim my poaching instincts in the least, and I have never been able, even at this late stage in life, to resist the urge whenever the opportunity presents itself.

I was, in later years, very successful with pheasants, so much so that I cleaned out the stock of one gamekeeper, but more of that later. Incidentally, it was on that same estate that I got my first stag. It was a Fallow Deer, and not an outstanding specimen, but it *was* a stag, and my ambition was satisfied for the time being.

I continued my nefarious operations, to the confusion and annoyance of gamekeepers in many parts of Scotland, for a long time.

Making my first acquaintance with rabbits was an interesting and fascinating experience, showing great potential, and opening up a whole new world for me. I also renewed my acquaintance with the 'trooties', but more of that later also. I must say that despite the enjoyment of my later escapades and forays among the game of the distressed landlords and gamekeepers on various estates, the thrill of the 'Red Legs' still remained uppermost.

If I was dim in school, I was pretty smart at learning when outside that torture chamber. I learned a lot from my father, but not by direct tuition. I just watched and listened to him. He knew a lot about poaching, but did not instruct or encourage me in that line. It was too dangerous on the island, but I believe he did indulge in this sport before he went there. He was reared in the Ardnamurchan area, and his father was drowned while poaching salmon, so it seemed to be in the blood.

There was very little my father did not know about boats and fishing, and the habits and behaviour of the lobster. He could almost think like one of those creatures, what they did and where and why. He also showed me where the lug worms were, and how to dig them up with the minimum of effort. If you did not bring one up with the first lift of the fork, he reckoned you were wasting your time.

I also learned from him the art of cobbling. Where he had learned it I do not know, but it was probably in the same way in which I was picking it up. He repaired all our footwear in a rough and ready manner. Rough it certainly was, but that was in keeping with the material being used, and the use to which the finished article was to be put. Hand stitching was a bit troublesome to him under the dim light of the paraffin lamp, and to put the waxed end through the hole made by the awl sometimes required the help of my keener eyes and more nimble fingers. But he needed no assistance when it came to knocking in tackets: he was a dab hand at that, and bashed them in with complete abandon until there was scarcely a tacketless area of leather to be seen. The 'maiden voyage' of those newly repaired boots was like walking on walnuts, until the more prominent tackets were battered or worn down to take their rightful place with their neighbours.

Cobbling and suchlike accomplishments were impersonal, and a pleasure to watch, and even to take part in, but hair cutting, another of my father's necessary accomplishments, was an entirely different matter — a ghastly, tearful and sometimes bloody affair. We would all be lined up, waiting our turn on the torture seat, listening to the strangled squeals of the current victim. Hair cutting was a major operation, the whole flock being done in one evening, as it was unthinkable that the whole shearing plant could be assembled and set in motion on a second night.

My father's hair cutting was on a par with his cobbling, efficient but rough and crude. An accidental snip on the point of the ear brought a sharp yelp from the victim and a copious flood of tears. Cries of distress and the wiping of the eyes added to the debacle. But the operation was carried through to a tearful conclusion, and the next in line called forward. Quite often this next customer would be in tears before the first snip, knowing what was to come.

Throughout the operation there would be shouts from the barber of 'Dhia! Can ye no keep yir head over!', and a clout on the head to indicate where he wanted it to be. A clout from my father's hand was not to be treated lightly, either. It was like being hit on the head with a bunch of bananas, for his fingers were permanently crooked and horny from years of rowing and hauling on ropes. As each customer was dealt with, the neck was liberally splattered with spittle as the barber blew lustily around that area to remove any loose hair that was likely to find its way inside the shirt. The insides of the ears were given the same treatment, and the customer was then free to stagger from his straddled position on the chair to the kitchen, where his head was held under the cold tap. This cold water treatment was supposed to condition the now exposed skull to any rigours which it was likely to encounter in its naked and vulnerable state.

Retrospectively, it may be amusing, but I would not appreciate one of those haircuts now, and maybe as a means of assuring myself that it will not happen, I have cut my own hair for the past thirty years.

There may of course be a mercenary angle to this, as it is highly probable that I have inherited my father's fetish for economy. Of course, he had every reason to be careful with his money, and in this had a worthy economist in his wife. My father's wage was never more than twenty-five shillings a week, and although there was a free house and an allowance of coal, waste of any kind in the household had to be rigorously guarded against. With a family of nine to provide for, there was never much to play about with.

As well as saving money, labour saving was practiced in the household. On the very rare occasions when we had a three course meal, my mother, with washing up in mind, would, after the soup course, call out 'Lick your spoons, there's pudding coming!' Needless to say, we licked smartly, in eager anticipation of a rare luxury. Our spoons were all-purpose, without any fancy designations, and it did seem pointless to wash and re-issue the same spoons for the same meal.

Venison, fresh in the shooting season, and salted and dried in the winter, was the mainstay of our diet, but when that ran out, we depended on our success at the fishing. If our catches were good, some of it was salted and dried out in the open air, to be used during the lean times, when stormy weather prevented us from getting the boats out.

Some of that dried venison was really hard tack, in the pure sense of the word. Choosing a suitable chunk, my mother would throw it on the concrete floor of the scullery, and lay into it with the hatchet. For quite a while there would be some doubt about whether the venison or the concrete would break first, but although the floor was deeply scarred and chipped by near misses, the venison invariably ended up in manageable portions, which were left to soak all night before being put into the big stew pot with swede turnips.

The venison, of course, was honestly obtained, and not poached. The venison shot by the Gentry was distributed to the staff, with the prime parts, of course, going into the castle kitchen. We all got the best pieces of what was left in our turn. The shoulder and the neck, usually damaged by shot, were considered the lowest grade, and the haunches the highest. We occasionally got our share of those haunches, though. Most of the gravy from the Castle kitchen seemed to come to us: the idea perhaps being that our seven children had to be kept well greased and running. Being the largest family, we always got more of whatever was going than the rest did, although it was largely the badly shot bits. However, whatever it was, it was always grist to my mother's mill, and would be salted and dried bone hard, ready for the lean times when it would be attacked by my mother on the concrete floor of the scullery. The heads and other offal, not fit even for the Camerons, were boiled down into soup for the dogs, and poured over the porridge they lived on.　It kept them quiet for a while.

The aroma issuing from the pot of venison stew, simmering on the open fire, although sometimes a bit over-mature, was none the less delicious, as it pervaded the house and met our sniffing and hungry snouts when we rushed in from school or play.　We did not question the ripeness of the meat, but the quantity of it, and after a few rumbustious hours among the rocks on the shore or scrambling over the hills, we were ready to eat the proverbial 'scabby-heided wean'.　Fortunately, we were never reduced to that extreme, but thoroughly appreciated and devoured all that was set before us, be it hard-tack venison or dried salt fish.　Keeping up our supply of fish was a more or less continuous operation and could be a pleasant way of spending a summer day.　In winter, it could be, and often was, a cold and at times dangerous operation.

Caves Bay was one of our favourite fishing spots.　There was a nice sandy beach where we usually went ashore and brewed ourselves a can of tea while we waited for the fish to swallow the bait on our long lines.　We got our water from a clear hill burn which cascaded over a cliff.　The same burn provided water for the puffers.　Those puffers were little coal-fired, flat-bottomed cargo vessels, which until a few years ago were common throughout the Highlands and all the islands, carrying all kinds of cargoes and usually being beached at high tide, unloaded onto the beach, and then floating off for their next port of call.　They were used to bring over to the island all the material for building the castle, and even the soil to make the gardens.

Near to the burn is the noted *Welshman's Rock*; of the Welshman there is no record, nor why he carved a narrow passage through the rock, as he is alleged to have done, several hundred feet above the sea.　To go through that passage is certainly a challenge to anyone who wants to test his nerve, and to anyone who is afraid to look down to the rocky shore, far below.　It is really a dangerous venture, as, when half way round, the adventurer is actually overhanging the edge, in order to negotiate a projection in the rock face.　Did the crafty

32

Welshman deliberately leave this projection to make sure that only the best and bravest got through?

Angus and I did it, but Kenny remained in the boat, just a toy in the water as we looked down. We did not dare tell our parents about our daring venture, as we would, most certainly , have been banned from that area. We were only schoolboys at the time, and a ban would have been fully justified. On our evening excursions we were usually accompanied by at least one parent, and then there was no time for nonsense like rock climbing. All our actions were directed towards fishing, and while the long lines were, we hoped, being loaded with fish, we carried on the good work with hand lines.

The return journey was always more interesting, as we usually had a good haul on board. There was also the added thrill of a race with any of the neighbours' boats who happened to be on the same expedition. We youngsters, none of us yet fifteen years of age, rowed our guts out for seven miles, while the old men (as we thought of them) lay back in the stern, puffing their pipes and shouting directions and encouragement. No rudder was allowed, as that would have hindered the progress of the boat.

If we did not want a jaunt, but merely fish, we usually set our line in the bay, directly in front of our houses. The bay, at that time, was seething with big plaice, up to twelve pounds in weight. This was quite a common weight, and we required a gaff to haul them on board.

After hauling our lines one evening, we paid a social call on an East Coast fishing boat which had come into the bay to spend the night. We were on friendly terms with all the fishing crews in the area, and never missed a chance of having a chat with them when they called. We would have been better to have given that particular boat a miss.

While we lay alongside, the crew gazed down, goggle-eyed at our catch, which covered the bottom of our small boat. When they had recovered from their amazement, I heard one of the men say to his neighbour 'Man, Jock, that would be a grand place for a trawl.' We had unwittingly disclosed the possibilities to those fishermen. That boat, and others who trailed them from Mallaig, where they had landed their poached haul, cleaned up our bay in a few weeks. They must also have ruined the breeding ground, as even now, seventy years later, not one fish of any kind is found in that bay.

Such destruction was carried out all up the West coast, but our bay was the only one that concerned us. It cut off our main supply of fish, even our main supply of food. We were then compelled to fall back on saith, a coarse fish, and not nearly as palatable as plaice.

Fishing for saith was cold and laborious work, frequently showing very little, and sometimes nothing, for several hours labour. It meant continuous rowing, trolling for the fish. I have rowed on a frosty winter's night until my hands were cramped and immovable around the oars. If we were lucky and the fish plentiful I would be constantly clouted across the face by fish swinging in on the rods. The hardship, though, was soon forgotten when we arrived home and filled the big pot with the fresh fish. We all had a cupful of the fish bree before starting on the more substantial part of the meal, possibly at one or two o'clock in the morning.

As I have said, fish featured largely in our diet, all the year round, and was never considered monotonous. In later years, my new fiancee got a good insight into how the rest of the world lived. Never at any time partial to fish, her first meal on arrival was fish. Perhaps romance supplied the sauce for this, as she did not complain. But she was horrified to find that the main meal for the next day, and for each day for the remainder of her two weeks' stay, was fish. By that time, romance was strained to the utmost. She eventually married me, but is still not keen on a straight diet of fish.

One of our methods of carrying our catch home was to tie one leg of the oilskin trouser with string, fill it with fish and sling it over the shoulder. It was a simple and easy way of taking our catch home, but one which, on a certain dark night, resulted in disaster. On our homeward trip, loaded leggings over our shoulders, we entered a narrow road leading to the farm steadings, and were met by a galloping and panic-stricken herd of deer which had been feeding on the turnips stored there. As the startled animals approached at full gallop, desperate to make their escape, it seemed certain that we would be gored or even trampled under their sharp hooves. But Angus was equal to the occasion. When the terrified animals were almost on us, he unslung his legging, full of fish, and swung it violently around his head. Flounders, saith, cod and haddocks were spread over a wide area, but the deer swerved frantically to avoid this strange barrage. It took us quite a while to gather in the catch from the surrounding shrubbery, but Angus maintained that some of the helpers' leggings were fuller after the mishap than they were before it. Angus was never at a loss for words to express his feelings, but on this occasion he exceeded his previous best, which was when he had been kicked by a bull. His lurid descriptions of the deer, the helpers who stole his fish, and the man who tied the leggings, were a joy to listen to in the dark.

Still on the subject of fishing, Sunday fishing was listed by us as the most deadly of the Seven Sins. Not so among the incomers, who were mostly Sassenachs, and uncaring of the beliefs of the Highlands. Despite dire warnings from the locals about the probable results of their breach of the Sabbath, a number of those Sassenachs set out on a fishing trip. Their trip was, apparently, very successful, and they had a good haul. Possibly they had no leggings in which to carry their fish, so instead they laced a string through the gills. Before coming ashore they decided to dip their catch in the sea, to give them a final polish before displaying them to us as they proudly bore them up the jetty. When they plunged the lot over the side of the boat the string broke and their total haul sank slowly to the bottom, from whence they had come in the first place. There was no sympathy from the locals who met them on the pier; only solemn faces, as they realised that their predictions, and their firm convictions, had been vindicated. It was a judgement and a stern warning to others who contemplated Sunday fishing.

Perhaps my son had not been told about this, or the warning had lost its potency. At about eight years of age, having made some acceptable excuse for not going to worship one Sunday morning, he was later observed, with the heathenly skipper of a puffer, enthusiastically engaged in this sinful and prohibited occupation, and right in front of his granny's window.   I have no recollection of the outcome of this incident, as, fortunately, I was not in the district at the time, but I have no doubt the reaction would be drastic and severe, and that he was treated as a leper for some time afterwards.

MY FATHER

My father, being, properly, the kingpin of the family, figures largely in my memories of our home life.   My mother, a hard working and somewhat self-effacing person, was born in Tolsta, Lewis, and brought up under the strict and narrow teachings of the 'Wee Free' church.   Consequently, she was anti-entertainment of any sort, spontaneous or otherwise.   She was not of the same rumbustious nature as my father, who would burst into songs, dancing or games of some sort, without any urging or reason, except that of his own high spirits.   My mother was almost constantly occupied with domestic affairs and the well-being of her seven youngsters, and but little interested in any of my father's bursts of exuberance.   She has not, I am afraid, left many strong impressions on my memory.

My father's forte was singing and telling us amusing stories, with quite often the joke on himself.   He gave himself, and us, a good laugh about the time he 'drowned' an unwanted cat.   Having carried out this unpleasant duty, he strolled slowly home, to find the cat drying itself in front of the fire.   He and we joined in the laughter, although today I wonder why.

I have always regretted that I did not enquire more closely into my father's early occupations and experiences before he came to Rhum.   He did tell us, however, about how he saved the boat on which he was working as galley boy when it got in among the rocks on a stormy night.   The skipper and the mate, deciding that all was lost, retired below to pray and, as he said, 'play with strings of beads.'   My father, the mere galley boy, not having his beads with him, and not knowing what to do with them anyway, set about saving the boat and himself.   His efforts were successful, and he steered the boat through the reefs and into smoother water.   The frightened men then packed away their beads and emerged from below decks. They assumed full charge and, once safely ashore, related their alarming experiences and their successful efforts to save the boat and the lives of all on board. There was no 'thank you' for the galley boy.

He also told us about his droving days, when cattle were collected from various areas of the Highlands and the Islands and driven to the Falkirk Tryst. That was the main market for the Highland cattle at that time, and the droving route went over the desolate Black Mount, and through Glencoe. All that the drovers carried in the way of sustenance was a little bag of dry oatmeal. When the cattle had been settled down for the night where there was suitable grazing and shelter for them, the drovers went down to the nearest burn with their bowls and stirred up their evening meal of oatmeal and cold water, after which they lay down in the heather beside the cattle.

If they were within reach of some inhabited spot, they would have a convivial evening with the local people, and have a 'reviver' which, I have no doubt, went down very easily after their long and often cold tramp across the moors.

My father told us that the best pick-me-up, after a hard day, was a glass of whisky poured into a pint of beer. We were not, however, encouraged to put this recipe to the test. Indeed, none of the family tasted beer or whisky until they were over thirty years of age. Now, so many years later, I can vouch for my father's statement.

After his marriage, however, the poor man's intake of alcohol was radically reduced. There was no strong drink available on the island, and the occasional imported bottle, under my mother's control, was carefully hoarded. She was, as with most forms of enjoyment, very much against strong drink, and rationed it out in a most parsimonious manner, usually after her husband had had a hard day out in extreme weather. When the grateful recipient downed his drink, in one short gulp, he invariably screwed up his face, giving the impression that it was horrible stuff, and warned us never to touch it, as it was very strong medicine, and highly dangerous.

Hogmanay, understandably, was the only time when we saw the head of the house slightly inebriated. All his cronies congregated in our house; the bottles went round, and the Gaelic songs rattled the roof. There was terrific jollification which we all enjoyed. It was a revelation to us to see those normally sober-minded men in a new light. My mother took little part in the celebrations, but sat back tight-lipped, for fear, no doubt, of having black marks jotted down in the Book of Judgement against her name. The entertainment would end in the small hours, with garbled good wishes for the coming year, and the revellers would stagger off to their various houses.

The next day would be spent sleeping off the unaccustomed revelry of the night, and that was it for another year.

To give but one instance of the brain-washing done by the Kirk on my mother when she was a child, I can recall one evening when we seven children were preparing for bed and were indulging in the usual rumbustious pre-bed games. On this occasion it was all unusually entertaining, and my mother, with tears running down her cheeks, was laughing hysterically. Suddenly she realised what she was doing. She wiped the tears from her face, tightened her lips and drew a long and solemn face. In a very serious voice she said 'There will be a judgement on me for this night.' She believed it too, and we were all quietened down and chased up to bed.

Fortunately, there was no Wee Free kirk on the island, nor indeed any other kirk, and although we were indoctrinated by hell-fire and brimstone teaching from missionaries from time to time, that was intermittent, and the impact it created was of short duration, and by the time the missionary reached us again on his rounds, his impact had lost much of its potency. The poor man had then to start his labours all over again, the labour of scaring the living daylights out of us. Gobbets of froth flew from his lips as he roared out about the reception awaiting us in the next world. Mrs. Macaskill, in whose house the meetings were held, maintained that the hens went off lay after the missionary's visits. Be that as it may, those sincere men did have some effect, however temporary. We were all affected in some way or another and it is difficult to imagine anyone who would not have been, for they were powerful preachers.

I remember that after each visit from the missionary, I myself was so affected that I decided to join the ministry in some form. Those earnest but hasty decisions each faded and disappeared in the course of time. Now I am as great a sinner as my neighbours, and have either lost my fear of, or perhaps have become reconciled to, my fate when I am slipped into the incinerator.

My injections of religious beliefs were too widely spaced, I fear, to have any lasting effect, but the visits of the missionary always rejuvenated the religious inclinations of our parents, for there they had a strong, even hereditary, foundation on which to rest.

After the missionary's visits, the psalm and hymn singing at home seemed to reach higher cadences, and the Bible was waved round more vigorously, as it took the place of a baton in my father's hand while he roared out his favorite psalm *The Lord is my Shepherd.* Meanwhile my mother, not being much of a singer, could be heard in the background, trembling and squeaky, twittering away.

In the fullness of time their enthusiasm would diminish until it reached a more normal level, where some of our infringements of the religious code were merely frowned upon, and we were chided instead of being skelped. Sentences could be severe in the 'stern' season.

I remember once being made to go down on my knees and ask forgiveness from The Lord. What was my sin? I had piddled on a hen that was confined in a wire-bottomed crate. The poor hen was also doing penance for her sins. She was broody and had stopped laying eggs, and as that was the only reason for the existence of the hen, this was the penalty, and she had to be brought back into line. Hens were not supposed to go broody. Their job was laying eggs, and to bring them back into production as quickly as possible, the accepted cure was incarceration in a draughty cage. This was meant to cool their bottoms and bring them back into the production line as quickly as possible. Part of the treatment was spraying with cold water. I could not see that a little piddling could do the hen any harm, and it might have hastened her return to productivity. But authority thought otherwise, and I had to pay.

I was more fortunate than a friend of mine, though. He and his pal had fallen out with a neighbour who bred fighting Game Cocks, and they decided to work out their spite against him by piddling on the Game Cocks.

It was hilarious to hear Davy describing, with embellishments, the operation. It was his turn to go first, but it was not too easy because the wire-netting was quite close meshed. To get a good jet where he wanted it, he had to penetrate the netting. If penetration was difficult, retraction was even more so, and before he could withdraw, the game cocks were on him and he had 'lost a ☆☆☆☆ yard of it.'

I must admit that praying was less painful than that, and who can blame Davy's pal for reneging when it was his turn.

Leaving the cocks and hens to attend to their own troubles, and going back to father, his education had been intermittent, at the best, depending on the weather, the season of the year and the state of the crops. This lack of formal learning was reflected in his reading and writing. My mother never had much time for reading, being constantly engaged in making or mending clothes for her large brood. She was, however, kept up to date with affairs of the outside world by my father, as he reclined on the sofa and read out the week-old news from *The Oban Times*. Not an exclamation or interjection would be missed out, and at times there would be joyous cries from the reader of 'Loud laffer and applause.' This was part of the article, and as such must be read out.

His hand writing was beautiful, and he was very proud of this accomplishment, but it could be alarming when he wrote letters as he was very impatient and needed a lot of help with his spelling.

With the writing paper on the table, he would be well into a letter to one of the family on the mainland. My mother, still busy with her knitting, would be arched and tense, waiting for her cue, which she knew would come several times before the letter was completed.

The cue would come as the writer waved his pen over the page. Glancing sideways at her, he would mutter the first letter or syllable of the word at which he was stuck. Mostly my mother would be quick to respond and spell out the troublesome word from that slender clue.

On one occasion the stumbling block was 'piano'. A piano tuner came twice a year to attend to the instruments in the castle and my father was giving the news to someone that the man was lodging with us. With the pen primed for action, he threw hopeful glances towards my mother, as he repeated 'P?---P?-----P?' My mother was unable to decipher this one, and as each 'P' became more peremptory than the last, she got more flustered. At last the writer's patience being exhausted, he roared out 'PIAAANA!'. My mother jumped, the cat jumped and the unwitting cause of the uproar, the piano tuner himself, was sprung from the sofa where he had been snoozing, quite unaware of the mounting tension and the impending explosion.

MORE OF MY FATHER

If my father was out of his depth in letter writing and reading, he had one natural gift that needed no prompting or tuition. He was a splendid tenor singer, with a tremendous repertoire of Gaelic and English songs.

He was always in great demand at all social events, but he told me that, on his first appearance on a public platform, in his native village of Acharacle, he was so shy that he stood with his back to the audience and sang his song through to the end in that position.

He must have had a most retentive memory, and the ability to assimilate what he heard, because he could sing very many Gaelic songs and quite a good selection of the contemporary English ones, despite the fact that there were no song books in the house, and he could not read music anyway. He would settle down on the sofa and, disregarding the absence of an audience, would sing his favourite songs, for the sheer joy of singing, but he was not left on his own for very long.

Gradually, children would drift in and gather about him, and not all of them his own. As many as could find room would squat on his body, and the others would crouch on the floor round the old sofa.

They did not much enjoy his sentimental or sad Gaelic songs, but they were patient, and knew there was more to come. Jogging them up and down on his knees, he would break into:
Crack, crack does my whip, I whistle and I sing.
I sit upon the wagon just as happy as a king.
My horse is always willing and for me I'm never sad.
There's none can lead a jollier life than Jim the carter lad.

There were several verses to that cheery song, each one followed by the chorus of *Crack, crack.......* in which the young audience joined. After a few more of those jiggity songs, he would start on what, I believe, was his favourite Scottish song, and a real tear-jerker it was.

That ballad, in my father's version — there are several others — told the story of a young maiden who was courted by two young men on the *Dowie Dens O' Yarrow*. A duel was arranged to decide the issue, but the maiden's brother, who did not approve of one of the suitors, *Went up behind, and stabbed him with a dagger.*

That was a cruel and treacherous act, and the singer gave it all the pathos and feeling of which he was capable. With tears streaming down his cheeks, my father would belt into the last verse:

Go home, go home, you false young man,
And tell your sister Sarah
That her true love John lies dead and gone
on the Dowie Dens o' Yarrow.

My father would give all he had to this moving ballad, and one could almost believe that he had been a witness of the tragic affair.

Completely overcome with emotion, he would lie back and wipe the tears from his face. After that moving performance, he seemed incapable of carrying on the entertainment, and the audience, somewhat sobered by the final song, would drift off to some more amusing pursuits.

My mother never sang solo, but I have heard her, while involved in her knitting or sewing, singing quietly a little sad story of *My Bonnie Wee Irish Boy*. This may have contained the flickering embers of an early romance, as she frequently mentioned the name of 'Mike Laffen', a man she had known before marrying my father.

My father was a very handsome man, and he knew it. An extrovert and quite a ladies' man, he never missed a chance of chatting to the women, and all those encounters broke up with roars of laughter.

Whether those social interludes had romantic undertones I cannot guess, but any transgression in that direction on the island was almost impossible. It was too close a community, and everyone knew what everybody else was doing, and where and when they were doing it. He was also inordinately fond of children, and would never pass a child without a bit of light banter which was always accompanied by much laughter from all those involved.

Christmas must have been an anxious and worrying time for my parents, and there must have been a tremendous amount of heart (and purse) searching, with presents to be picked and priced for seven children from a weekly wage of not much more than one pound. Those gifts had to be picked from a catalogue and ordered from Glasgow.

Those catalogues were a great joy to us as we turned the pages and gazed at the wonderful things displayed there. We made our selection of the toys we would like, knowing full well that there was no chance of any miracle happening and that all we could do was gloat over the unobtainable. We knew, of course, that such things existed, and thought they must have come from some fairyland of which we had no knowledge.

I remember once, after having scrutinised all the articles in the catalogue, and having given them all up as fit only for dreams, we got together and each one gave his or her idea of what would be the ideal gift. Our lust for what we thought of as luxury food, and the fact that it was unobtainable, was reflected in our choice. The majority of us opted for a whole barrel of apples to be set beside their chair, and to be allowed to sit there until the barrel was empty. Needless to say, we never got our barrels of apples. In fact, for some reason which I cannot now explain, we were never given apples at any time. On special occasions we were given one orange (part of the loot brought home from some party and stashed away) divided among the seven of us. One wee segment each, which we made last a very long time.

The most memorable of the parties from which those treats came was the one given by the Doigs, to which our family was the only one invited. Willie Doig was the electrician, and he and his wife were childless, but both were very fond of children, and they laid on everything to ensure the success of the night.   The one-eyed host — as short as his wife was tall — was a good pianist, and to his own accompaniment would entertain us with rollicking, humorous and silly songs, which I think he made up as he went along.

Jamsy jee ma jibbery oh, jibery ohry pory.

Ikey pikey sikey crikey, jinny go vallipa dora.

Silly, it was, and with many more verses, but good fun for us.   Those were really memorable nights, which would be spoken about for many days, and the next one eagerly waited for.

Unfortunately, one of those parties ended on a very tragic note.   The prohibition on keeping dogs had been relaxed (so long as they were very small dogs), and we had been given a Skye terrier pup, which was our greatest joy.   Of course it did not go to the party, but was left at home, to enjoy itself as best it could in the dark.   On our return from the party we waited at the door while my father went in to light the big lamp which hung from the ceiling in the centre of the room.   As he walked across the floor, matches in hand, the puppy, bounding with glee, raced forward to greet us, and in the darkness my father trod on it.

Within a few minutes the pup, our friend, was dead, and all the joy of the party was forgotten as we mourned over the wee, white, lifeless body.   We missed the pup sadly, and wept over our loss, but with the resilience of youth, the tragedy was soon forgotten, wiped out by the distractions of the festive season.

This pre-Christmas period was a time as exciting for us as it must have been worrying for our parents.   The list of selected items had to be sent to Glasgow, and after that everything was in the hands of Providence, and of the McBrayne's steamer *The Plover*.   There were quite a few things at risk, but in matters over which he had some control, my father was taking no chances.   On the pretence of going to visit his friends in the bothy, he would casually meander out of the house, leaving us sitting around the fire discussing in hushed tones what our stockings might contain in the morning.   They were now draped along the front of the mantlepiece, a long line, flat but promising. Some younger hopefuls, not pleased with the size of their own, had replaced them with my mother's stockings, leaving no excuse for Santa Claus. The filling of those long black bags would certainly present him with a problem, but it was a problem he usually overcame with balls of fancy coloured paper that pleased the eye as well as filling the stocking.

Suddenly we all froze. Faintly in the distance could be heard the tootle of a bugle. With bated breath, mouths agape and all eyes staring at the ceiling, we listened as the sound grew louder, as if passing overhead, and then fading away into the distance.

Slowly we relaxed and turned to each other. 'Did you hear that? Did you hear him? That was him! He went right over the house! Will he come back?' In hushed voices we discussed the phenomenon, as we waited for our father to come in. When he did saunter nonchalantly in, whistling a merry tune, we exploded on him, and with voices strangled with excitement and emotion, poured out the whole striking event. 'Did you hear him, Papa? Did you not hear him? He went over the house!' With a solemn and innocent expression he would reply 'No, I didn't hear anything, but I thought I saw something flying over the house.' This fully convinced us, and as we crept in 'awed silence up the stairs, we were sure that our stockings would be full in the morning.

But if, for whatever reason, the *Plover* had not made it that year, there would be no bugle in the sky, nor anything else. In the case of such a disaster everything was brought into play to give the impression that someone had, at least, called. Some little objects would certainly be in our stockings, but not quite what we had expected and hoped for.

My mother, poor soul, would scurry around, making little twitters of excitement, as she drew our attention to 'finds' in various corners of the house. There would perhaps be a mutton bone, with quite a bit of meat on it, behind the door, where 'he' had dropped it on his way out. An orange that had dropped out of his bag, even a scone with plenty of butter and jam on it, and even a few rare sweets were found by my mother, who excitedly drew our attention to them. 'What a careless man he must be,' she would say, 'To pick up and drop these things as he rummaged about the house.'

Somebody's trousers would be be tied in a knot, so 'he' must have a sense of humour. All these diversions quickly made us forget our disappointment over the missing toys, toys we had hoped for, but never really expected to get. What a worrying time Santa Claus and his wife must have had, trying to put on a show for us, from the little they had.

We were not a bit envious of our friends' toys, when we saw them in daylight; after all, anyone can hang a popgun on the end of a bed. There was nothing personal about that, but we had positive proof that 'he' had been in our house. We described in detail all his movements in the house, where he had been and what he had dropped on his rambles through the house.

It was indeed a vivid picture that our parents portrayed, and we could follow Santa's every move, as if we had actually been present during his nocturnal ramblings.

All the indications of a mysterious visitor were accepted by us, and were more appreciated and certainly more thrilling than the expensive junk lavished on my grandchildren today.

I do not believe in Santa Claus now, but I do believe in a father and mother who, during those anxious and frustrating times, made every effort to ensure that their children had all the thrills and beauty of the Christmas season. They had few material gifts to present us with, but what little they did have was lavished on us, liberally sprinkled with love and joy.

The truth was revealed to me when I was about ten years old. On my way to school I had looked through the mail which was littered about the Post Office, waiting to be picked up by the recipients. Among the assorted boxes lying around was one with our name on it. It did not look like the usual monthly box of groceries, and my interest, if not exactly my suspicion, was aroused. At first my mother denied all knowledge of the mysterious box. However, my persistent pestering eventually compelled her to admit its presence, and I was let into the secret. Of course, I was sworn to secrecy, and accepted my share of the loot at the hand-out, with a smug air, and an inward feeling of superiority, as I watched my young brothers and sisters displaying their gifts from Santa Claus.

All those little gifts and surprises meant a lot to us. Modern children are continually fiddling about with money, and have lost all sense of values and appreciation. We never had any money, and in fact did not need it, for there was no shop on the island.

The Post Office sold the bare necessities for existence, such as bread and large sea-biscuits. We very rarely bought bread, and if we did, treated it as a luxury, and as a special treat were given half a slice on Sundays. All our scones, oatcakes and barley bannocks were made at home, a week's supply at one big baking. All our sweets (various kinds of toffees and candies) were also made at home. My mother even made ice cream, and no substitutes were used, only real double cream and beaten eggs. There was no fridge, of course, so our home-made ice cream was a winter treat. On a very cold day, the basin full of mixture would be placed in a large bucket and set out on the drying green. The bucket would be packed with frozen snow and left for the mixture to freeze. With keen anticipation we watched it from the window until my mother brought in the bucket and divided the mixture, frozen hard by now, into seven wee blobs. Only seven, for the seven children: our parents contented themselves with licking the spoon clean.

My father was the confectioner. On a wet Sunday, unable to take us for one of our favourite walks, perhaps to the Child's Grave or to the Round House (a derelict house on the hillside, one of the many ruins left by the eviction of the crofters), he would set to with some of his own recipes and secret mixtures. His concoctions did not last long, and were always finished long before the next wet Sunday. Those confections of his were the only things we ate that did not contain oatmeal. All other dishes contained oatmeal, which he considered the essential ingredient to give them the final touch of perfection. No matter what my mother was cooking, he invariably butted in with 'Give it a sprinkling of oatmeal.'

Chewing seems to be inherent in children, and we were no exception. Our parents could not make chewing gum, so, as in all other situations, we were obliged to make the most of what was available. In this case it was cods' eyeballs! They made a satisfactory substitute. Stuffed cods' heads was a fairly common dish, and there was always keen rivalry for the eyeballs after the head had been boiled. They resembled small white marbles, and flaked off gradually in the mouth. With careful sucking and manipulation, an eyeball would last all day.

Sucking cods' eyeballs assuaged our desire for sweetmeats, and was not addictive, as smoking would have been — had we been able to get our hands on anything to smoke.

I do not think that chewing the eyeballs was the cause of one of my companions becoming addicted to nicotine, but it certainly gave him a push in that direction.

Willie, one of my good friends (and also my opponent in many things) one day tried to beg an eyeball from me, but I was not giving any away that day. In a spirit of bravado, he then decided to do something more exciting than chew eyeballs: he would smoke, and he would show us how to do it.

Tobacco was unobtainable, and was quite out of the question, but that did not deter him. He was a determined lad, was Willie, which I will show in another chapter. Scouting around, he came up with the very thing to suit his purpose. That was a piece of the withered branch of an elder tree, from which he extracted the dry pith. He then bored a hole through to where the pith had been, and was ready for action. He lit a match, applied it to the hole and took a big sook. The effect was startling, and the expression on Willie's face did the operation full justice as the live flame shot up the tube and into his mouth. When, smartly, he took the tube out of his mouth, there seemed to be a rod of fire projecting from somewhere around his tonsils.

Smoking was there and then excluded from Willie's curriculum. Well, it was temporarily. After his tonsils healed, Willie went on to bigger things, and eventually became a seasoned and hardened smoker of Thick Black and Bogey Roll, filched from his father's stock. Those were the two most popular brands on the island, and they were sold in the Post Office, alongside the stamps and postal orders. This of course was beyond Willie's means, as he was, like the rest of us, penniless. He was therefore compelled to maintain his supply from his father's stock. The awful stuff came in rolls like tarry rope, and smelled really vile when being smoked. Willie was a determined beggar, and although he was sick several times in my presence, he persisted, and survived to a good old age still smoking his Bogey Roll.

Willie's reckless, determined and indomitable spirit came into its own when he was among horses. Having mastered the questionable joys of smoking, he was now addicted to horse riding, and would mount anything, broken or unbroken. In fact, the less broken they were, the more he preferred them. Could the nicotine, coursing through his veins at that early age — he was not yet fifteen — have had something to do with his reckless behaviour? I have seen him catapulted between the hames of a fully harnessed horse at full gallop. Only the intervention of providence could have prevented him from being impaled on the projecting spikes.

Set him on a sledge behind a half-broken horse and he would tear along the road in a hail of stones from the animal's hooves, any one of which, if it caught him on the head, was quite capable of braining him. But that reckless, fearless boy, yelling his head off, would lash the beast on to even greater efforts.

Willie was in charge of the garden horse and cart, and even this outfit had to travel at maximum speed when Willie was on the road. He was sent one day for a load of cow manure, this being considered the best top dressing for grape vines. Willie was a bit late in arriving with his load. When he did, eventually, arrive with a sweating horse and full load, he announced proudly that as he was unable to get any cow manure, he had brought a load of bullshit! Willie's load was accepted as a commendable effort from the male of the species, and Willie was highly complimented for his initiative.

While I dealt with the delivery, I could hear in the distance the rattle of the cart as Willie galloped off for another load of — well, something.

To be in charge of a galloping horse, as Willie always seemed to be, can be an exhilarating experience. An uncontrollable galloping horse, however, is an entirely different experience, as I found out. A beautiful black horse called *Soldier* had been, supposedly, fully broken, and was being taken for a final run yoked to the jaunting car. Young Angus, Old Angus and I were the passengers, while Duncan held the reins. We had just passed the Post Office when the horse bolted.

It was the greatest sensation of speed I had ever experienced, and as the wind tore at my eyes and hair, I was quite bewildered by the telegraph poles swishing past in quick succession. I was enjoying the ride immensely, and did not realise that all was not as it should be, until Old Angus jumped off and splashed into the river.

The horse had the bit in its teeth, and Duncan's efforts to control it were quite unavailing as it tore along, even seeming to increase its speed, leaving Angus to scramble out of the water, his cap floating past him.

Duncan was doing his best to prevent the horse taking the right angle bend, over the river and into the stables. He was pulling hard on one rein in a hopeless effort to make the animal go straight up the Kilmory road. The horse had other ideas, though — he was for going over the bridge and into the stables, and no man was going to stop him. Maybe Willie could have done, or he would have died in the attempt, as we almost did. The galloping horse turned sharp right, and the jaunting car hit the corner of the bridge with a shattering crash.

In a moment everything was splinters of wood, wheels and horses hooves. My next recollection is of trying to make my way through a thick holly hedge enclosing a close wire fence. In the midst of my struggles I seemed to hear my father shouting 'What are you doing here? Get away home at once!' I do not remember going through the hedge, but I did, and undoubtedly it was in an effort to escape from the carnage on the bridge. I have no recollection of doing so, but I must have scrambled my way home, as I came back to reality the next day, lying in bed with a big bandage round my head. My memory of the actual crash is a bit hazy, due, no doubt to the crack on my head, and I sometimes wonder if my reckless and irresponsible behavior in later life was the result of that clout. The other two passengers were not seriously injured, but Duncan was very badly knocked about, and spent many weeks in hospital and on crutches. *Soldier* was sold off, very cheaply, to a crofter in Skye, and never gave any more trouble. I have no doubt that the animal glimpsed something, perhaps imaginary, through the long mane that covered his eyes, and panicked.

MY MOTHER

Unlike poor Soldier, I did not prove to be tractible and well-behaved. If someone said that something could not be done, I was always the clown who attempted to show that it could be done, even at the risk of life and limb.

The jaunting car experience, which had proved to be no jaunt, was just one of the escapades which seemed to afflict entertainment and pleasures outside the home. In our own little family circle, safe from the dangers of the outside world, we had our own harmless diversions.

There was always a lot of chit-chat and what might be called *wise-cracks* amongst the family. Many of these, so many years later, are still repeated, and still give us pleasure whenever the company seems to be flagging.

We had a pet lamb once, which gave us a lot of pleasure. It had the run of the house, and took more advantage of this concession than it really should have been allowed. It also caused some embarrassment to my sister Mary, embarrassment which she was not allowed to forget for a long time. Being the oldest of the family, she felt it her duty to keep an eye on the youngsters, and see that they did not get into forbidden mischief, and she had appointed herself chief custodian of the store cupboard. She tried to make sure that we youngsters did not eat the sugar and jam when mother was not about.

My mother had a jar of currants which she kept in the sideboard, and on these Mary kept a very watchful eye, as we would, when the road was clear, snatch a handful and be off, often, in our haste, leaving a trail of evidence.

One day, full of the importance of her position, and with something of importance to report, Mary took my mother over to the sideboard and pointed to the evidence on the floor. 'Look, mama,' she shouted, 'Someone's been stealing the currants.' My mother took a close look at the 'currants', and saw that they were the result of liberties taken by Topsy — the pet lamb was indeed a pet, but was not house trained.

But Mary got her own back on Iain, who was tormenting her about something, probably the 'currants'. Mary snapped 'Away you go and wash your face. You're filthy.' Iain, knowing well that fishermen are always dirty, chiefly because there is so little fresh water for them to use for washing when at sea, claimed that he was a fisherman, and therefore justifiably dirty. Mary's retort was smart and to the point, as she told him 'Well, if you are, you surely don't need to carry the bait in your ears.'

But this was children's talk, and it was my father who was responsible for most of the memorable sayings, sayings that we still quote with relish to each other when those of us who are left meet. For some reason, some peculiar quirk in his make-up, he used a sort of oral shorthand in which he would use only the first letter or syllable of a word. He spoke of *su* instead of sugar: instead of the lavatory he always referred to the *'lava'*.

Our 'lava' was at the foot of the steps leading to the back door, and when my father was ensconced there and found no convenient paper in sight, we would, quite frequently, hear his long-drawn cry of 'Paaaaap'. If the back door happened to be shut at the time, his frenzied calls must have been heard in the middle of the village.

When the calls eventually impinged on my mother's ears, she would scurry hither and thither in desperate efforts to find some of the urgently needed material. Paper of any kind was quite a rare thing with us, and it was usually *The Oban Times* which provided the necessary supplies for the 'lava'. It was unthinkable for us to mutilate or desecrate any issue of this, though, until the next one was available. Consequently, the search for paper could be not only urgent but sometimes quite desperate. It would be a combined operation, all ages being conscripted for the search, opening cupboards and drawers, feeling under chair covers, peering into dark corners. During one of those really quite frequent hunts, my mother pushed her hand under a cushion and struck, well, not gold, but, under the circumstances almost its equivalent. It was something that at least felt like paper. Trusting to her sense of touch only, she hauled the material out and with a 'Here, give him that' shoved it into the nearest waiting hand of the 'Lava Courier Express'.

The calls ceased, and there was silence for a few minutes. Then we heard the back door opening and the slow steady steps of the master of his flock. But it was not a majestic figure that approached. My father was holding up his trousers with one hand and in the other he was carrying what appeared to be a sheet of cardboard. With an injured and pathetic expression, he looked round the room and enquired, in a quavering voice 'What sort of stuff is that? It would take the skin off an ELEPHANT'S backside!' It was years later before it occurred to me that very possibly my mother knew perfectly well what she was doing that day.

We children played, or fought, among ourselves, as most children do, while my father took his ease on the old sofa, or perhaps danced and sang, as the spirit moved him. My mother, like all mothers of those days, seldom had any leisure. She was always busy, with sewing or knitting if nothing else, but occasionally she would sit back and dream, mostly, I think, of her past life and early romances. She would then, after a few minutes' silence, sit up and chide herself for her idleness, and get on with whatever she had in hand at the moment.

My mother had been born at Tolsta, on the Isle of Lewis, and had had the very severe upbringing usual in that place, where the Kirk was both extreme and powerful. Pleasures of almost every kind were frowned upon, and this had left its marks on my mother, who always found it difficult to relax and enjoy herself. She had left home at a very early age to follow the herring and work as a fisher-lass, gutting and packing the fish in virtually every herring port round the coast.   Eventually she had come to Rhum as a maid in the White House, where the gentry lived before the Castle was built.   She was the cook there when she met my father, already working on the island as a ghillie and boatman.

Sometimes she would amuse us with incidents and stories from her early life.   She told us of the wonderful life at the sheiling on the hills, where the cattle were taken to graze all summer.   Boys from the various crofts acted as herds, while the girls busied themselves with milking and making butter and cheese.   When there was enough of it, this was carried home and sent off to Stornoway to be sold or bartered.

The youngsters who were not at the sheiling joined the peat cutting squad, which consisted of all the able-bodied from the the community. That was very hard work, but they were a happy bunch, lightening the labour by singing and joking on the sun-warmed moor.

Peat cutting depended on the weather, and as no fine weather could be wasted, it was a full day's outing, from dawn to dusk in the long summer days.   Baskets and creels were taken to carry the peats home, with *crocans* to boil the tea.   Stories from the elders of the company would enthrall the youngsters as they munched their hard tack of oatcakes and barley bread, thickly coated with their own homemade butter.

Each family guarded its *crocan* very carefully, for those old tins with wire handles produced tea the like of which there never had been before or since.   The ash from the fire, and the bits of half-burned heather that had to be fished out from the thick, boiling liquid, all added to the delectable flavour, so my mother said, and it was grand to sit there up on the hill with a full *crocan* while the old ones told their tales.

But there was no fun and games when it came to carrying home the product of their labours.   That was really horses' work, only there were no horses.   The peat banks would be anything up to a mile from the houses, and the peats were carried in large creels or baskets, with a strap round the forehead of the bearer.   Ploughing through bogs and leaping over water-filled drains with a heavy load supported from the forehead was no joyful canter over the moor in the summer sunshine. And yet my mother's sister, when she was seventy years of age, was still doing such labour, as lean, sure-footed and nimble as a deer. Those people were all sustained and nurtured on the products of their own hard work, but, ironically, many of them died at a healthy old age. , If they escaped the illnesses of childhood, then it seemed that they lasted, and lasted in good health, for many years.

My mother also told us how she and other girls followed the herring fleet, gutting the fish and packing them down in salt in the barrels. They were paid very little for that miserable, cold and dirty occupation, but it was the only work available, and the money it brought in, however little, was very necessary at home. There was no way of earning money at home: therefore it was the herring, until many of them went into domestic service, as my mother did and eventually arrived in Rhum.

One day she told us a really 'dirty' story. It concerned a gamekeeper, who might have been called Mac. His popularity had become a bit tattered, owing to his habit of appearing most afternoons, and asking for, indeed almost demanding, food, and then retiring to sleep it off in the girls' bedroom. After a bit of thought, the girls arrived at a solution.

One day when Mac arrived for his usual meal, they had it all ready for him, starting with a big bowl of broth, liberally fortified with a good dose of Jallap. Now, Jallap was a very powerful laxative, one found in every house on the island, and indeed, I believe, all over the Islands and Highlands, where it was held to be a good cure for most ills. I can vouch that it was good for coughs, because after a dose of Jallap you were simply afraid to cough! Anyway, Mac seemed to enjoy his meal, and then went, belching with satisfaction like some Arab, to the bedroom to sleep it off.

Having got him settled down, the girls shut the door, quietly locked it and went out for the afternoon. They returned several hours later, full of apologies, saying they had forgotten all about him, and had locked the door to protect him from any unauthorised intruders. Mac

58

thanked the girls for a comfortable afternooon, and left, leaving the girls somewhat mystified about his seeming composure. But despite his composure, Mac had been alarmed. He never came back. Clearly he had smelt a rat.

After he had gone, the girls did a bit of investigating, and were no longer mystified. When they opened one of the drawers, it was not a rat they smelt. The Jallap had done its work in the usual robust style, and so had Mac. But the girls said it was almost worth it, just to get rid of Mac for good and all.

Kirsty's fervent wish was *'Tha mi'n dochas gu bheill toll a thonn eir a losgadh.'* Kirsty was a good-living woman, and not given to swearing, but her outburst on that occasion, everybody felt, was fully justified. I am not going to translate it, and everyone who can read it will be more amused than offended. Those who don't have the Gaelic can have it translated for them, and then, if they are offended, have only themselves to blame. It might even encourage them to learn the Gaelic, and that would be a credit to Kirsty.

There was another good story told by my mother, which gave us a good laugh, but which caused my father to cringe with embarrassment. My mother and Kirsty were employed at the White House, and at the same time my father and his friend Angus were the only occupants of the new bothy, which had been built for the bachelors employed there.

Having been indoors all day, the girls decided that it would be nice to have a stroll in the cool of the evening, and it was, I am sure more by design than chance that their stroll took them close to the bothy, and I have no doubt that they made no efforts to conceal the fact that they were there, as they strolled along, giggling and chattering on their way up the field. The two young men had gone to bed, wearing only their shirts, as most working men did in those days, and at the sound of the chattering girls passing their bothy window were instantly alert and decided to give them a surprise, and themselves a bit of fun.

So it was out of bed and out of the window, still just in their shirts. The girls showed very satisfactory signs of alarm as they fled up the brae, the brave boys in hot pursuit. But the girls had their minds on a bit of fun, too.   When the men were almost on them, they turned and raced towards them.   The pursuers were now the pursued, and the brave lads, shirt tails fluttering in the wind of their passing, flew back over the stubble.   Together they crashed against the window, and crashed through, like two rabbits into a burrow, my mother claimed.   They had certainly put the best foot (and other parts of their anatomy) forward, but had lost a lot of face, and the hysterical laughter of the girls made it impossible for them to make a second appearance.   In the fullness of time, however, their wounded pride was healed, and eventually they married the two girls, and it was no longer necessary for them to chase each other about the fields at night.

Of course, we had our outdoor activities, diversions and escapades, some of them entertaining, some of them painful.   My mother's attempts at rearing eider ducks could, I think, be classed as entertaining.

Eider duck eggs were a highly rated bonus in our annual safari for seagull eggs, and were considered a great delicacy.   There was never any doubt about what you had found when you came on an eider duck nest, one of those much sought-for treasures.   When the duck left the nest, frightened away without having had time to conceal the eggs from predators (and we were predators), she emptied her bowels as she took off, and the stink of that mess was enough to daunt all except the most hungry and hardy predators.   We were of the first category. As a matter of fact, we were alerted by the smell.   It has been stated in some books written by naturalists that the bird regurgitates this mess.   That is not so: I have guddled about so much of it, picking out the eggs, that I have no doubt which end it comes from!

We always tested the eggs in the nearest water to check on their freshness, and on one occasion, at my mother's request, took home a clutch which we considered to be in the first stages of incubation. She was going to rear eider duck as an addition to our lean economy.

The first batch we took home was fairly successful, up to a point.   Ducklings did hatch, and were allocated a small pond near the henhouse, but their wild and natural instincts prevented them from acccepting this, and although the pond was not in sight of the sea, they immediately set off in the direction of their natural element, cheeping along in single file, with the poor old hen which had hatched them trotting along at the back and frantically calling them to come home. We headed them off, and then fenced them in, but it was no use. They spent most of the day doing no more than just gazing through the wire in the direction of the sea. Eventually, and in not too long a time, they died off, perhaps from a surfeit of the garden worms on which we fed them.

But my mother was not disheartened. She had got so far with the first lot that she was sure the next lot would be a success.

In preparation for this new attempt at duck rearing, the dross was swept to one end of the coal cellar and then the prospective mother, knowing nothing of what was before her, set on another clutch of what we hoped were fertile eggs newly taken at a considerable and smelly effort from an eider's nest.

Unfortunately, the only hen that seemed to be interested in hatching eggs at that time was a White Leghorn. They are notoriously poor sitters, but, since nothing else was available, she was co-opted, and the results were awaited, with patience and hope, by my mother, and with fortitude by the hen.

We really didn't know anything about the incubation period of eider duck eggs, nor did we know the age of the eggs we had found, so it was decided to leave the whole affair to what we thought would be the superior knowledge of the White Leghorn, but that was misplaced confidence: she had no more idea than we had.

After what seemed even to us to have been an inordinately long period of incubation, the hen's nerve, or it may have been her enthusiasm, finally broke. My mother was still hopeful and expectant as she opened the cellar door one bright summer morning, quite expecting to hear, as she expected every day, the cheerful 'cheep cheep' of young eider ducks. What she got was a completely mad and totally *black* hen, in full flight, and emptying her bowels as she flew, screeching and yelling her way to freedom. She disappeared over the dyke, and was not seen for several days. The wretched creature had broken all the eggs, which were in an advanced state of decomposition. She had then taken a dust bath in the coal dust. When my mother opened the door, she got a belch of rotten egg gas and, from both ends of the thoroughly frustrated hen, a vivid expression of its view of duck eggs. When my mother had cleaned herself up, she echoed the sentiments of the hen, and indeed seemed to be quite sympathetic to her. Enough was certainly enough, for both of them, and that was the end of trying to rear eider ducks.

An incident like that, although perhaps it did not afford the major participants much pleasure, certainly gave us a lot. There was one incident, however, that is more amusing in retrospect than it was at the time.

It would have been an amazing and even an alarming sight to any observer who did not know what was going on. And even if he had known what was going on, he would perhaps hardly have believed it.

Seven children, ranging in age from about two to ten, cringed in the corners of our large room, the younger ones in obvious fear of what was happening. There was a large table in the middle of the room and around this rampaged and crashed a large dog, straddled by a large man, my father, holding it by the tail. The man was moving backward and the dog, frantically, forward, and this made both traction and direction somewhat uncertain, particularly as the man was trying desperately to stand still, while the dog tried desperately to keep moving. To say that their movements were erratic would be an understatement. They bounced off the corners of the table and scrambled about amongst the upturned chairs, while, on the fringe of the arena, my mother darted hither and thither, like a demented hen looking for a lost chicken.

She rattled about among the dishes on the shelves and operned cupboards and drawers in a frantic search. And the search was indeed frantic as the cries of my father became more imperious and demanding.

'Mustard,' he cried, 'Bring the mustard!'

It all began like this: there was a collie dog owned by Donald Ferguson, an elderly shepherd living at Harris, seven miles away. The dog had been smitten by wanderlust, and invariably arrived at our house, where we children made a great fuss of it. Donald instructed my father to catch the dog the next time it appeared and put a good plaster of mustard on its backside. This, Donald assured my father, was a certain cure for truancy in a dog.

That explains the performance, the desperate cries and the equally desperate search by my mother for the potent ingredient. The search, however, was in vain, and my mother announced, in a trembling voice, that there was no mustard.

This would have stumped many men less single-minded than my father. He was equal to the crisis, though, and, quite undismayed, changed his cries to 'Bring the pepper. Bring the pepper!' I am quite certain that he had no idea of the potency of pepper, but, having caught the dog, something had to be applied.

Not many people, I should think, have attempted the operation of peppering a dog's backside, but anybody with even an elementary knowledge of the topography of a dog will realise that this was not an operation to be undertaken lightly. It would not, of course be very effective if the stuff was thrown just anywhere about the hindquarters, with the unfortunate animal in a horizontal position. No, quite clearly the animal had to be hoisted at least semi-vertical and the cure applied liberally under the root of the tail, where, it was hoped, it would really sting — if there was any sting to it.

Despite vigorous protests from the dog, the performance was concluded, to the satisfaction of the rider, if not of his mount, and the animal was released. The door was opened, and the beast was off, via the kitchen and the pots and pans. The resulting clatter as they hit the floor must have convinced the poor beast, if he needed any more convincing, that the very devils of hell must be residing in that house.

He was holding his tail down, very tight, as he disappeared over the hill, but I do not think that the effects of the pepper, if indeed there were any, could have lasted long, because he was holding his tail very high, as usual, when he returned a few days later. He had learned at least part of his lesson, because he would never come into the house again. We children thought that a pity, because we never got the chance of testing Donald's theory. By then we had discovered the elusive mustard, but first you must catch your dog.

SOME ISLAND CHARACTERS

Modern children have their 'Dr. Who', and other such trivia, but we had our shepherds (Donald of the wandering dog was one of them) and other worthies who provided us with a lot of our entertainment and thrills, some of them tragic and some them of mysterious. There was Donald, for instance, who arrived in the village very early one morning and said that he and the rest of his family had been aroused during the night by showers of stones being thrown on to their beds. Now, Donald was not an easy man to scare, and he had lived in the house at Harris, seven miles from the village, for many years, and I know that he did not walk seven miles, in the early hours of the morning to report the disturbance without some good reason. Donald's arrival, and his story, caused a bit of a stir in the village, but I have no recollection of the outcome of the incident.

The first man Donald made contact with when he arrived with his strange story was Duncan nicknamed by us youngsters 'Dingley', for what reason I do not know. It is very doubtful if Dingley made any sort of investigation into Donald's troubles, for the man had enough troubles of his own.

Dingley was the farm manager, and although he was never stoned, like Donald, he easily could have been, or knifed, for that matter.

As farm manager, it was his job to find out, from the French chef, what meat was required each day for the gentry in the castle. I listened to one of those confrontations, and it was just as confusing to me, who was not concerned, as it was to poor Dingley. He could speak no French, and the chef could speak very little English. On the occasion I heard them, the chef seemed to be saying 'Bodderax, wee, wee, Bodderax', and to this day I have no idea what it was he wanted, although plainly it was some sort of meat. Even Dingley could gather this, and he nodded his way out of the affair. He went off, muttering 'Bodderax' to himself, 'Bodderax, aye, aye, Bodderax, well, well.'

The chef, as usual, would get a bit of a cow or a sheep, but what bit it would be, Dingley had not yet decided.

Those chefs were highly mercurial, their tempers strained to breaking point, working in front of the huge open range, among the steaming and rattling pots and pans. I was one day almost run down by a fleeing kitchen girl, pursued by an infuriated chef waving a large kitchen knife.

We did not really laugh at the plight of poor Donald, who had been stoned out of his house, but there was another shepherd who did give us a good laugh, and there was nothing mysterious about him. Ruaraidh lived at Kilmory, five miles from the village. He was not very tall, but was extraordinarily well built. His thighs were so enormous that when he was walking, his feet were about eighteen inches apart, yet he thought nothing of walking the five miles from his house, just to have a chat with someone.

But Ruaraidh could do more than walk. He was reputed to be a very good runner, and was spurred on to take part in the Highland Games which were held in the Castle grounds every year. That was fine, and Ruaraidh was willing enough, but he had no running pants. The call went out 'Ruaraidh wants pants!', and the search resulted in my father discovering a discarded pair, part of the strip of the Rhum Rovers, a football team of which my father was at one time a member. He had been one of the 'stars', or even 'heroes', as players are so inapppropriately called today.

Ruaraidh, hearing of the discovery of this sartorial treasure, walked the five miles to our house for a dress rehearsal, and walked home with a bounce in his heels and a small bundle under his arm. He was delighted with the outfit, despite the fact that, at the preview, they resembled a new skin and were glistening with tension. Ruaraidh was certainly pushing his luck.

Ruaraidh was one of the first runners out on the line that day at the Games. He was out there limbering up, and proudly showing off his running pants while the rest of the runners were still finishing off their cups of tea.

The gun went, and Ruaraidh was off to a good start.

He was going well, leading the field, and with every indication of being the winner. Then disaster struck. He was taking a bend at high speed, leaning into it like a ship under full sail, when the blue pants split, right down the middle, and now, instead of the blue pants, of which he was so proud, glinting in the sun, it was poor Ruaraidh's naked backside that flashed past. During the race, you could have sworn Ruaraidh was at maximum speed, but he wasn't. He only reached maximum speed after his pants split, and he left the course, going like a leopard for a convenient clump of bushes. For a few moments there was no movement from the bushes, and during that time, I have no doubt, he was assessing the damage. He must have decided that the damage was extensive, and so, with no hope of making a dignified exit, his head appeared above the foliage, and he semaphored for trousers.

Ruaraidh's moment of triumph was over, but he got a standing ovation from the large gathering of gentry, of all sexes, who had witnessed the disaster. It was Ruaraidh's first and last appearance at the Rhum Highland Games, but he was not forgotten.

Another shepherd was 'Johnny Come Over', who lived with his wife and two small children in a wild and desolate place beyond Caves Bay. He caused a commotion when he failed to return home after collecting his monthly supply of necessities from the steamer. Johnny was fond of a dram, and it is sure that part of his 'necessities' was a bottle of whisky.

It was a dark and stormy night when he set out to walk the five long miles across the moor, and when he failed to turn up at home, his wife raised the alarm in the morning. A search was made, and Johnny's body was found. His sack of groceries was found first, and beside it an empty whisky bottle. It seemed that he had drunk his supply of whisky, and then wandered off, over the moor, until he stumbled across a telegraph pole. He took that as an unprovoked attack on himself, and he challenged the pole, and spent the rest of what was left of his life battering it with his fists. He was found, in a trampled ring of mud which he had made round the pole. There was blood on the pole, and the bones of his knuckles were exposed.

Nobody could tell me how he had come to be given the name of 'Johnny Come Over', but it was the only name he was known by on the island. Whatever the explanation for the name, Johnny had come over for the last time.

There was a story told me by my father about a shepherd who had lived in a distant and most inaccessible part of the island. Within the shortest possible time, his wife had given birth to four children, and none of them had been baptised. It was at last decided that the time had come for that deplorable and even dangerous state of affairs to be ended, and it was arranged that the minister would go across that lonely moor and do what was necessary. On his arrival at the house, after a well-earned rest and refreshment, a basin of water was produced, and the multiple christening got under way. The minister approached the basin, carrying the infant and followed by the parents and a toddler, holding on to its mother's apron strings.

The minister was one of the old fashioned kind, who did not believe in half measures, and made sure that everything was done with the utmost conviction. He was liberal with the water (there was plenty of it in that place, anyway!) and he gave the baby a good slosh. This unexpected douche was too much for the infant, who gave tongue in a lusty manner.

It was also too much for the toddler, who had been a witness to the 'assault', and, releasing his hold on his mother's apron, approached his father. Looking up, he whispered ' *'m bual miu'm bucair, Pappy?'* Or, in English, 'Will I hit the bugger, Pappy?'.

The minister, perhaps used to such outbursts at rural christenings, ignored the interruption, and, glancing round, enquired as to the

whereabouts of the other two prospective participants in the ceremony. A search located them in the utmost corner, under the bed,
from which refuge it was found impossible to extract them.

The man of God, with thoughts perhaps of his long walk back over
the hills, and possibly still smarting from the outburst from the toddler,
caught him by the neck and with a 'You get in there, too, mac an
Diabhail' (son of the devil), threw him under the bed with his brothers,
and then, grasping the basin, sloshed the contents under the bed, at the
same time intoning 'In the name of the Father, the Son and the Holy
Ghost, I baptise you Alexander, John and Malcolm.'

My father assured me that his story was quite true, and we had no
reason to doubt it. In fact, I would say it was highly probable,
because those children rarely saw any other human being but their
parents from one year's end to another, and were as wild as young
deer. They would scurry into the outhouses at the sight of a stranger,
and remain there, until the intruder, and disturber of their peace, had
vanished.

Another noteworthy shepherd was Sandy Nicholson, who lived in
Guridale. This is a smooth-sounding word, and should be pro-
nounced 'Gyouridale' and not, as I hear it today on the island,
'Gurridale'.

Guridale is, in my opinion, the most peaceful and secluded place on
the island. Sandy lived there with his wife and several children. He
was a morose character, with a big overhanging moustache which
seemed to be a hindrance to his attempts at conversation. Indeed,
those attempts were rare, and he seemed to be the butt of his
associates, especially at clipping and dipping times, when, with all the
men on the island gathered together, it seemed that everybody had a
stab at him.

He was a sturdy man, and I have seen him set off to walk the six
miles home with a hundredweight of oatmeal on his back. But more
of Sandy later.

Mention of oatmeal brings to mind our provisions, and our efforts to
get them. At times, when they were almost within our grasp, the

steamer would be seen sailing by, carrying away for another week the foodstuffs of which we were often badly in need.   If the Captain of the *Plover* decided that the seas were too high for him to attempt the entrance to our loch, that was the end of it.

Frequently, coming home from Oban High School, where my sister was continuing her education, the steamer would be unable to call at Rhum, and the only Rhumonian passenger on board, my sister, would be dumped on Eigg, to make the best of her way home from there.

When the storm, which had prevented the steamer from calling at Rhum, had finally subsided, my father and a friend would row the fifteen miles across that dangerous strip of water to bring his daughter home.

They had some rough crossings, and often enough Mary would have to bale continuously until they reached the shelter of the cliffs of Welshman's Rock.

Such experiences, however, were part of our existence, and added a little spice to our lives, giving us something to talk about for a few days.

When the steamer had failed to land our provisions, the borrowing runs would start.   Children would be seen running from house to house, with their little bowls for a 'Wee bit sugar, a wee taste of tea, oatmeal or flour, till the boat comes in.'

Perhaps the smokers suffered the worst hardship.   Those poor unfortunates would scurry about, seeking and searching.

I have seen my father, in dire straits, go to the rag bag and retrieve old waistcoats destined for the tinkers.   He would spread them out on the table, disturbing colonies of moths, and go through all the pockets, meticulously shaking out any dust or debris there might be there from the more salubrious days when he had parked his pipe in those very pockets.   Whatever he recovered by such salvaging, and I think it was more bits of pocket than bits of baccy, would be mixed into various recipes, obtained from the morning meeting in the stables, where every brand of pipe fuel could be smelt.

Some favoured dry beech leaves, while others sang the praises of dockans. Each of them puffed away, and each praised his own particular blend.

The man was fortunate who, when his wife's attention was elsewhere, could raid the tea caddy. This caused a good bit of envy, but the culprit had to be careful, because the smell was very distinctive, and his wife could scent, from a hundred yards away, her precious tea literally going up in smoke.

One of my father's tasks, in the off season, was that of ferryman, a most arduous task at times, which frequently entailed rising at three in the morning to meet the steamer, which would be well out in the bay.

The skippers of the steamers were always a bit wary of going aground on those dark winter mornings, and lay well out, putting a considerable strain on the ferrymen who had to row out to meet them. And, what was very much worse, row a perhaps heavily laden boat back.

We would all be alert, from a very early hour, watching for the light which was hoisted at the post office to indicate that the steamer had left Canna. My father would then don his oilskins and sou'wester and make for the pier.

It was no pleasure jaunt for him and John MacCaskill to row the heavy ferry boat, with its huge sweeps, out into the bay on a stormy winter's morning.

At least twice they were unable to row the boat back to the pier, and stayed anchored out in the bay all day, in full view of the houses. For long periods, as we watched anxiously, the boat would be hidden by spindrift and rain, and then we would be relieved to see them again, when the squall had passed, still anchored there, still rolling and bobbing in the same frightful way.

Another of my father's jobs, when he was not ghillying, was supplying the castle with fresh fish and lobsters. This could also mean many rough sea trips, when he and John MacCaskill would row many miles out to the banks in the Sound of Rhum, and spend the

71

whole day there, fishing with hand lines.

They usually took their food with them on such occasions, and a bottle of cold tea: there were no thermos flasks then.

On one occasion there was a near crisis when my father found that he had left his pipe at home, and was unable to puff as he fished.

The day was saved, though, as after a bit of scrounging around for a substitute, he eventually pounced on one of the freshly-caught lobsters, and after a bit of careful knife work, removed one of the big nippers, broke the point off it, scraped out the flesh, filled the the claw with tobacco, and he was off. The fishing was more than just bearable after that: it was almost enjoyable.

Two of the crew of the *Rhouma*, thinking that it would be a nice change from scrubbing decks and polishing brass, volunteered to do the fishing. They were not going to do it the hard way, though: they took a sail.

They were back by midday, without a fish, and in a state of shock, loudly proclaiming that as far as they were concerned, the position was open to anyone who wanted it. They said that a large sea-serpent, or some similar beast, had surfaced near their boat, and that the creature reared up in three loops, or arches, through any one of which their boat, with mast and sail, could have passed.

As nothing like that had ever been seen in the waters about the island, the volunteer fishermen had to stand up to a bit of ridicule. I noticed, though, that neither John MacCaskill nor my father, the most experienced boatmen around, pointed any finger of scorn at the two would-be fishermen, and I have often wondered about that.

Those two men from the *Rhouma* were both experienced Skye seamen, and not easily scared, so I am convinced they must have seen 'something'. And it was not drink talking. Taking into consideration the background and age of the men, and the fact that they refused what they thought was a sinecure of a job, certainly something had given them a considerable fright, and that in itself was enough to give a certain credence to their story. I well remember one of the

Kinloch Castle, Rhum

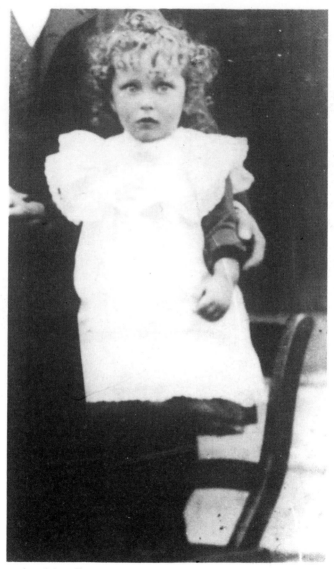

Archie Cameron yesterday

Archie Cameron today

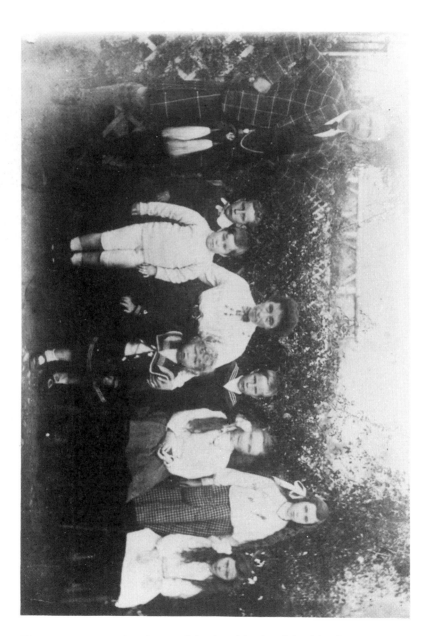

The Cameron family, with Archie beside his father

Croft Ruins at Kilmory, Rhum

Two inhabitants of Rhum today

Archie's father in his Sunday rig

A view from Kinloch Castle

Archie Cameron's Mother and Father

The Mausoleum,
burial place of Sir George and Lady Monica

men concerned, 'Red Angus', a tough Skyeman, of about sixty years of age, and if anything frightened him, it was no fairy.

I myself have spent many days in that same area, miles from the land, and the only creatures that annoyed me were, believe it or not, midges! Despite statements by the naturalist pundits that those insects are never encountered off-shore, I have seen them actually at sea, on many occasions. When a slight breeze ruffled the water, they could be seen diving under the thwarts to shelter there until all was calm again, when they would flutter up to resume their lightsome frolics.

Of course, they were Rhum midges, indomitable, insatiable and fierce. Of the species, this breed stands out unchallenged and alone. They are, without doubt, the Supremos of the midge world. I should know, because I have been the basic diet for millions of them.

Another source of food, apart from fish, was braxy sheep. Braxy is a bacterial infection of sheep, and in those days usually fatal. But it did not affect the flesh, and since only the best and fattest sheep were struck down, to find a newly dead braxy sheep was a find indeed, and a great help to the diet of the lucky family.

I cannot vouch for its authenticity, because I have never seen it in operation, but it was said by the pundits that, on finding a dead sheep, the finder should grasp it firmly by the hind legs and swing it round his head. If the legs withstood six full circles, then the sheep was fit to eat. Be that as it may, there is no doubt that a promptly-found braxy sheep was 'wholesome fairin'. Any over-ripe specimens were inclined to stop the breath, but no more so than 'hung' pheasants or grouse, which left a mound of squirming maggots on the larder floor. If the gentry could enjoy their hung pheasants and grouse, and ungutted snipe, why could not we, the lower echelon, enjoy the occasional braxy sheep?

On at least one occasion, we did not even have to look for the braxy sheep on the hill. The 'hoggs' or young ewes were usually sent to winter on the mainland, as the island winter was considered too extreme for them.   On one of those trips two of the beasts died of braxy.   They were in prime condition, and so were promptly given the last rites, which consisted of skinning and dressing.   A rope was then smartly attached, and they were towed behind the *Kinloch* all the way to Kyle, were they were taken on board, liberally salted, and taken back to Rhum, to provide more than a few good dinners.   Certainly, well pickled and salted, braxy mutton was a grand change from the usual diet of salt saithe.

When the braxy and venison ran short, it was always back to fish, usually saithe or plaice, and the favourite was plaice, until the Mallaig trawlers discovered their bed and left us without a single plaice for the rest of the time on the island.

Fishing for saithe was a lengthy, painful and sometimes unrewarding occupation.   If the shoals were on the reefs, we had a good haul, and frequently enjoyed a potful of them boiled when we got them home, at any hour after midnight.

The actual fishing for them, though, especially on a cold winter night, was anything but a pleasure trip.   If the fishing was good, and you were on the rods, the excitement kept you warm enough, but for the poor chap at the oars there was little pleasure or excitement.   He was constantly being clouted round the head with cold, flapping fish: his feet, usually bare, would be immersed in cold salt water and fish, and his hands were cramped and almost frozen on the oars.   He dared not stop rowing, though, as long as the shoal was there, and the lures of white feathers or sheep wool must be kept moving.   Yes, a lot of our fish was hard to win from the sea.

Fishing for plaice, on the other hand, was in comparison easy and pleasant, especially as we did it in the bay right by the village.   With a hundred-hook long line down, we could be sure of getting a good catch of very large plaice, and fine eating they were.

We youngsters often had a lot of fun in fishing from the pier when the young saithe moved in, like shoals of sprats.   This was mainly for fun, and hardly added anything to our food supply, except on one occasion when we saw, as the tide receded, that a large shoal of young saithe had been stranded in a pool.

This was no time for rods or any other sort of finesse. We were in amongst that shoal in a moment, determined to have every last one before the tide came back to release them. The youngest amongst us were chased off home, to get every possible container they could find — and some very strange ones appeared. We scooped at those fish until there was not one left, and then we hurried home, each with a fair haul to present to our mothers. The little fish were washed, rolled in oatmeal and fried crisp and brown, heads, fins, tails and all. What a feast!

As a matter of fact, I almost had pneumonia after that display of the primitive hunter instinct to attack anything that moves. We had been up to our waists in cold sea water for a long time that day, and a lot of us went down with colds. Mine 'turned bad', but the illness came to nothing, frightened away perhaps by the generous applications of camphorated oil, goose grease and 'Antiphlogistin Plasters' and thick brown paper that went on to my back and chest. and stayed there until I was well.

Some of our diversions were risky and dangerous, I now realise, but no-one had ever thought that fishing off the pier held any risks. However, one day when I was hurrying down there to join the lads, I met Willie on his way home, followed by his elder brother Neil. Neil was holding his rod tip high, as though he was still fishing.

I stopped and asked if the fishing was as bad as that, since they were going home early. 'No,' replied Neil, 'The fishing's good. Have you a knife?' I had, and produced it from my pocket. Well, it did resemble a knife, and certainly had opened many a mussel, and showed it by the amount of grime still sticking to the broken blade. Eagerly Neil took it, wiped it cursorily on the backside of his trousers, and got to work on Willie's ear. It appeared that during one of the casts, the line had slotted neatly between Willie's ear and his skull, and in the forward cast, the hook had become firmly embedded between the ear and the head, quite spoiling what Neil was sure would have been a champion cast right into a school of saithe.

Neil reached for his brother's ear, pulled it away from his head and made just one quick slash. The hook was revealed and was neatly lifted out. Willie grunted and jerked his head, but Neil was not in the least sympathetic, and upbraided the hapless lad for getting in the way of the line. A bit of pressure on the wounded ear to restore it to its approximate position, and it was back to the pier for more fishing, stilll with Willie hanging about, but this time well in the background.

Of course, not all our spare time was spent in fishing, and at least once Angus created something of a sensation with his spare time activities. He helped himself to one of the four-inch shells, a relic of the Boer War, which was on display in the tower by the roadside. Angus bore this object home in triumph, and decided to see what was inside it. His sister was an interested observer, and together they crouched over the shell while Angus struck at it with a hammer. There is no record of how many times he hit the shell, but what is on record is the the fact that the shell exploded, making a large crater and showering them both with gravel, although, miraculously they both escaped any other injury. The rest of us hardly needed to be warned again about playing with shells, but, in any case, the temptation was removed by the tower being locked against all future intending shell demolishers.

Angus did not explode any more shells, but he was a rambustuous boy, always up to some harmless mischief, and giving us a lot of amusing entertainment. He was tall for his age, and had big feet for his height, and so we called him 'Ship of the Desert', especially in the summertime, when he ploughed along the roads, raising clouds of dust.

He was a thorn in the flesh of Angie, the horseman. Angie never knew what was in store for him when Angus was on the loose, and lived in a state of tension whenever he saw the lad hanging about, usually with a wide grin on his face. Somehow, despite his awareness, Angie was never able to circumvent or avoid the new crisis that Angus had thought up.

It was one of Angie's jobs to be at the pier, with his horse and cart, ready to move any goods that arrived on the steamer. He did not like hanging about the pier on cold wet days, and he did not like his horse doing it, either. Consequently, he always left the harnessing of the horse until he heard the steamer blow as it came into the loch. If his timing was right, and it usually was, he arrived at the pier just as the ferry boat was drawing alongside. It was here that Angus threw spanner after spanner into the works.

There was the time when Angie heard the steamer blow, and quickly parking his pipe, which he had been peacefully puffing, unaware of the crisis ahead, he hastened to the harness room, to find all the bits of harness securely nailed to the wall. The oaths, threats and imprecations that flew from Angie as he furiously attempted to remove the harness were really blistering. Angus was almost hysterical, his face poking out of the loft as he watched and listened to the furore down below, at the same time keeping a wary eye on the bolt hole in case things went wrong.

Angie wrenched madly at the harness, leaving bits of straps and leather hanging from the nails, and, salvaging what he could, left gobbets of foam on the horse's flanks as he cobbled together what harness he could from what he tore from the nails.

Angie took steps to guard against this harrowing experience happening again, by harnessing the horse well in advance of the steamer time, and thus, as he thought, leaving nothing hanging about that might incite Angus. But Angus was patient, and bided his time, waiting for a really wet day.

He did not have long to wait, of course, and on this particular day, Angie had the horse harnessed in good time, but had made the mistake of leaving his oilskin coat and sou'wester hanging on the wall. This was just what Angus had been waiting for, and he had made his preparations. He was already in the loft, waiting for the spectacle. Angie reached for his oilskin coat and plunged an arm into the sleeve, to find that the cuff had been securely tied, and the sleeve filled with sheep droppings. If Angus had been near, he would certainly have been impaled on a pitchfork, for Angie had a vicious temper. And

77

yet, after he cooled down, Angus and Angie were good friends, and spent hours together in the harness room.

But Angus was a proper young devil, certainly. It was he who put a lump of gelignite in Old Sandy's soup pot, and sent the beef up the chimney. He was a big strong chap, but academically no great shakes: I was in the lower grade of no-hopers at school, but Angus was below me.

His main interest in life, apart from plaguing Angie, was internal combustion engines. Even before he left school at fourteen, he could diagnose any fault in an engine, and correct it in minutes, to the confusion of the experts. Through a bit of influence, he got a job in the Berges Engineering Works in Glasgow, and finished up as Chief Engineer on the Directors' yacht. Unfortunately, he was killed in a street accident in Liverpool, and I lost a good friend.

Angus's lack of formal education prevented him from taking his proper place among engineers, but the faults and failings of engines, and the alleviating of them, was ABC to him. When others, much more highly qualified, would dismantle an engine to diagnose its faults, Angus would simply listen, and seemed to do his diagnosis by intuition.

Like all the other lads who left Rhum to start work in Glasgow, Angus lived there with relatives who were prepared to sponsor him until such time as he was able to suppport himself. It was expected, of course, that the lodger would supply whatever he could to assist in his keep. It was therefore certainly expected that the lodger, returning from his annual trip home, would be laden with whatever good stuff the island could provide, such as eggs, fruit, fowls and vegetables.

I remember one occasion when Kenny and I, who both worked near Glasgow, were entrusted with a rope, several feet long, of home made white puddings. (Whenever a sheep was killed, whoever reached the slaughter house first, carrying a bucket, was entitled to all the internal tubing from the nose to the tail. Those tubes were an essential part of the pudding with which Kenny and I were entrusted.

There must have been some fast runners in our family, because we always seemed to have plenty of tubes.)

The trust put in Kenny and I, though, was quite misplaced. Kenny and I arrived in Glasgow empty-handed. We had started on those long feet of white puddings before the train left Mallaig, and when we reached Crianlarich there was not an inch left. It must have been quite a shock to our relatives to find that we had travelled light.

While Angus was the master of the internal combustion engine, Angie, his friend and sparring partner, was the one who was called for when it came to dealing with animals, especially horses.

Every year the wild ponies were brought in from the hills, where they lived unattended, and a selection made for the annual sales in Oban.

Naturally, those ponies brought a higher price if they were even half-broken. Also, the working ponies on the island often needed to be replaced, and the replacements came from those wild creatures brought in from the hills. It was Angie's job to do this. Old Sandy was, without doubt, the strongest man on the island, but the job with the ponies needed more than strength: it needed nimbleness. Angie had both strength and nimbleness, and also determination in plenty. He was the only man for the job.

He was a small sturdy man, accustomed to working with animals, and never prepared for the devious ways of young Angus. But any beast that had evaded, or even attacked anyone who approached it, was fair game for him. The determined wee man, teeth grinding, and his eye on the horse that was marked out for breaking, would charge into the middle of the herd and grapple the animal to the ground. The ensuing melee was enthralling, and it was at times difficult to distinguish man from horse as they thrashed about in the dust of the enclosure. Even the other animals stood around, and gazed in astonishment at the spectacle before them. But when the snorting had become panting, and the dust had swirled away, it would be seen that Angie had won again. He would be lying on the animal's neck, with two fingers stuck up its nostrils, completely in command.

A halter would then be fitted to the animal, and Angie's work was half done. The animal would be harnessed to a big trunk of wood, big enough and heavy enough to prevent the pony from breaking into a gallop. It dragged that around for a good while, and after that came the harrows, and with the beast by now in a lather of foam, it was considered incapable of trying any fancy tricks. But those Rhum ponies were tough, and the harrows seemed only to revitalise them. I have seen the animal, which, a few minutes earlier, had seemed to be completely exhausted, gallop across a ploughed field with the harrows bouncing behind it. Angie, too, hanging on to the reins, would be galloping for the first few yards, but then he would be down flat, the tackets in his boots gleaming and his chin leaving a bow wave in the soft soil. That performance would last for about two rounds of the field, until the horse found that towing the man and the harrows was more than he could manage. He was by now completely subdued, and showed no fear or even resentment as his conqueror went up to stroke his heaving flanks, pat his neck, whisper into his ears and blow up his nostrils. Angie might have had to spend an hour, or even two, conquering the horse, but now he had to gain its confidence. He knew well that horses are not 'broken', but only tamed: a broken horse is a ruined horse.

Angie's work with the animals did not end with breaking the wild ponies. When it came to getting animals on to the ferry boat, and then slung up on to the steamer, Angie was again the star performer.

To those animals, a boat was foreign ground, but Angie coaxed them gently down the slipway, over the pier and then induced them to jump down into the boat. To watch him doing that was to have a full appreciation of his ability to handle animals. If one of them lost its footing on the slippery floor boards of the boat, Angie would be down there immediately, getting it to its feet and calming it down.

Occasionally cattle as well as ponies were exported, but bulls or ponies were all the same to Angie. He would be down amongst them until the ferry boat drew along side the steamer, and there he attached slings to the animals and they were hoisted on board, to the cries and directions of Squeaky, the captain of the *Plover*.

The bridge of the steamer was high above where the slinging operation was carried out, making it necessary for Squeaky to turn on maximum voice volume, and the more the volume, the squeakier his voice got.

A bull was being slung up one day, under the interested gaze of a large audience of passengers, of all ages and sexes, and there was Squeaky up on the bridge, waving his arms and in an increasing crescendo of squeaks exhorting the sling operators to 'Mind his balls! Mind his balls!' I suppose most of the tourist passengers would accept that as part of the atmosphere of the islands, and as something to relate when they got home.

But Squeaky Robertson, captain of the *Plover* for many years, was a wonderful seaman, who knew the west coast, its perils and its possibilities as few other men did. If he said the Plover couldn't go, she didn't, and neither did any other ship. The old *Plover* was a top-heavy tub, but he could handle her under the very worst conditions.

What he could not do anything about, though, was the passenger accommodation. There was first class, and that was minimal. For the others, there was the cargo hold, and I have seen women and children tossing about down there in the most incredible conditions of dirt and discomfort.

Any animals being transported were tethered in the same part of the ship as the third class passengers used, and the stench and ordure in which they had to endure a long and, at times, stormy sea voyage, was incredible. There was vomit and cow dung everywhere, and it was almost impossible to avoid it when passing through that veritable hell hole. A lot of those poor wretches had to endure that from Barra, culminating in what they all dreaded, the rounding of Ardnamurchan Point, before the run into Oban, where they staggered ashore, more dead than alive.

The crew of the steamer were all from the islands, and did their best to alleviate the suffering of those people, but there was quite simply nowhere else to put them, as, quite often, the waves were sweeping the decks.

Angus and I made one memorable trip. We ensconsed ourselves in what we considered a sheltered corner of the deck, but, within minutes, the wind changed, and the waves were sweeping into our corner, even though we were on the upper deck.

Nobody knew we were there, and consequently no-one came to our assistance. We dared not let go of the railing for fear of being swept away. While we held on, grimly, cases of lemonade swished from one side of the deck to the other, but we dared not let go even with one hand to reach for one of those fabled bottles. In a strange way, although without doubt we were both desperately frightened, we enjoyed that trip.

The importing and exporting of cattle, sheep and ponies was always interesting, and never happened without us being there. It was a break, a big exciting break in a life that had very few such breaks.

Most animals being brought on to the island were unceremoniously pushed over the side of the steamer, and allowed to make their own arrangements about swimming ashore. The more valuable animals, such as pedigree stallions and bulls, would be pushed off the steamer and then roped to the stern of a dinghy and towed ashore. That is what happened to the white stallion imported by Sir George in an attempt to improve the native breed of pony. It did not last long on the bleak winter hills. Less important animals, having been pushed into the water, were simply pushed around, pointed in the general direction of the shore, and left to get on with it.

Invariably they did, and would then be collected over a wide stretch of shore line. After a day's rest, the sheep would be dispersed to their various hirsels, and driven off by the four shepherds — Murdo, the head shepherd, to Kilmory, Sandy to Guridale, Donald to Harris and, to the wildest and most remote hirsel, Dibidale, to which there was no road, by Johnny Come Over.

Stags also were imported from the English parks, and they certainly left their mark on the indigenous deer, which had become a scraggy and inbred lot. Following the introduction of those Sassenach stags, there was a marked improvement in the local breed, and one beast, when grassed, weighed in at twenty four stone, believed to be a record.

The heads of some of those specimens are still on display in Kinloch Castle, and a magnificent and imposing display they are, each one bearing a brass plate indicating where it was shot, and by whom.

It is a picture, somehow, of a just retribution, as the heads of those once noble animals gaze down, seeming disdainful and scornful, over the graves and mouldering headstones of those who shot them. Gray, in his *Elegy*, caught the spirit of it all, and I will not try to emulate him.

It would have been more fitting, perhaps, had there been permanent mementoes of the shepherds and of their wives. They were note-worthy people, and should be remembered.

The men would be fully occupied, roaming the hills, attending to their flocks, but their wives must have led lonely lives in those isolated areas, with no contact with any other woman unless they undertook a walk of at least five miles over the moor. Babies were born in those places, without any assistance from the outside world, yet as far as I remember, all those babies survived and thrived lustily.

Occasionally, relatives from the distant mainland would visit them, and their arrival, and that of many others, must have been as alarming to them as it was entertaining to us.

If the tide was suitable, a horse and cart would be drawn alongside the ferry boat and the visitors transferred to that. That was luxury transport.

At other times, with no cart available, the lady visitor would be carried, piggyback, to what she hoped was dry land. This would at times fall short of her expectations and hopes, when the piggy, underestimating the weight of his load, or overestimating his own ability, would dump her short of dry land, to loud lamentations of ruined stockings and shoes bought specially to cause a sensation among the rough and primitive natives.

With more favourable tides, the ferry boat could come alongside the pier, to which was fixed a vertical ladder. The ladies protested loudly, but there was no other way of getting their fancy shoes to dry land. The whispered comments of the men holding the boat steady would be either critical or appreciative of the climber's underwear.

'Look, Sandy, they're not bloomers! They're short ones!' 'And silk stockings, too, Angus.' 'Aye, Aye!' 'And did you see the fancy suspenders?'

These remarks were, to say the least, informative, and gave us an understanding of how the fancy city ladies dressed. The observations were of course relayed in Gaelic, with urgent jabs of the elbow, as the two men, with exaggerated helpfulness, made sure that the climber's feet were secure on the rungs, until they were out of reach. I suppose they looked on those benefits as part of the perks of the job, and much preferable to having a *cailleach* (old woman) on your back at low tide.

There was one hilarious day, though, when Duncan was detailed to deliver a cailleach to the beach. This old lady had, for easy transport, draped herself in all her clothing, and, wearing a long black skirt and two coats, she resembled nothing so much as a big bundle of old clothes. But she was more big than bundle, as Duncan found when she was hoisted on to his back. Duncan simply collapsed slowly and inevitably into the sea. Fortunately, it was not all that deep, and the only injury was to the cailleach's dignity, as she waded ashore, holding her clothes high. Duncan refused all future consignments.

One of the ladies who was helped up the ladder, I particularly remember, was one of my teachers. A pretty wee thing she was, and very prim, and she found climbing up the ladder very undignified. She would have found it more undignified could she have understood the comments coming from below about her 'short ones'.

We took her out in the rowing boat one evening, for a cruise round the point.   We were quite a long way from home when she asked to be put ashore, for an obvious reason.   My father, reluctant to interrupt the easy motion of the boat, suggested that she take the bailer up the bow, to which she replied: 'Indeed, and do you think I am a beast of the field?'   So we put her ashore, and she disappeared modestly behind a large and convenient rock.

She it was who once lifted Kenny's kilt, skelped his wee backside and rocketted him through the red curtain which divided the school room from the church.   Altogether, it was quite an imposing building, but the division between the religious and the secular was strict, and was marked by the red curtain.   We in the school room were at least shielded from the awesome sight of the empty pulpit glaring down at us.   Only on the rare occasions when a real minister called at the island would the red curtain be drawn aside, revealing the full imposing size of the room.

However, the punishment for any deviation from the strict discipline of that particular teacher was to be bundled through the curtain into the religious side.   It was a real punishment, too, for the empty pews seemed to be full of ghosts, and, even apart from the austere look of the pulpit, the atmosphere was redolent of disapproval.

Missionaries were not permitted to use the church.   Perhaps the holy place would have been defiled had an unqualifed preacher occupied that pulplt!   The missionaries held their second-class services at the McAskill's house, where they let rip, with complete abandon.

I remember one man, a huge man he was, with plenty of wind space.   There would be flecks of foam on his face before he was even properly into his sermon.   I have heard many orators, but none to equal that man in his ability to roar out the words from the very base of his belly.   He was a genuine and dedicated preacher, and left no doubt in anyone's mind about where they were going if they did not mend their ways.   The whole atmosphere reeked of sulphur.

It was obvious that the congregation had been duly impressed, and on leaving the house, spoke in whispers, casting furtive glances around, lest they be caught unawares, and swept into that eternal fire on which the holy man had laid such emphasis, before they even had the chance of getting home, making amends, and repenting. Within a few days, however, everybody would be back to their cheery, (and maybe sinful) way of life. The dogs would bark and the hens would lay!

The three successors to Miss McNab, who skelped Kenny, were a little more friendly than she was, and more easy going. One of them so much so that she went off on leave and came back much slimmer than when she left. Who could blame the girl? Entertainment was almost non-existent, and the occasional visit of a naval patrol boat was an event to be taken advantage of: it might be a long time before the next one called.

Our lady teachers were followed by men, of whom I have nothing but sad and painful memories. They were, however, I believe, both very clever men, even if sadistic and truly evil when under the effects of their personal devil, which in each case was alcohol.

One of them taught us navigation to a very advanced stage, and we became so proficient at semaphore that we could read all the messages being transmitted ashore by any naval vessels that might be anchored in the bay. Fortunately, this particular man had a wife, who was able to take his place in school when he was on the bottle. Often enough we would meet him, this unfortunate man, when we were walking to school. He would be unshaven and collarless, making his way through the village, begging for drink. We were young, and ignorant of the effects of alcohol, but knew by the whispering of the adults that there was something sinister about it.

That was a likeable enough man, when sober, but he was succeeded by another whom I can describe only as a fiendish genius. He did much, though, to help my sister win her scholarship to Oban High School, where she was found to be two years ahead of others of her age.

Both those men were highly qualified and worthy of much higher positions than the ones they held, but they had been banished to the island, where no drink was sold, in the hope that they would be able to overcome their addiction.   But somehow, they managed to get what they craved, somehow, and by any means, however expensive or undignified.

SCHOOL

School! The happiest days of one's life? Not of mine! The only happiness I got from school was the walking there, but even that was not with any anticipation of pleasure. In this case, it was certain that it was more pleasure to travel (even without hope), than to arrive.

I knew there would be no pleasure at the end of the trail, but the walk across the sands of the bay, barefoot, as we always were from April to October, was pure joy. If it was low tide, we made a collection of razor fish,which we placed on a shelf under our desks. Periodically we would bob down, squeeze one of the shellfish until he popped out, and bite a bit off. They were very tender and sweet. While crossing the sandy bay, we would trample over the empty shells of oysters, all that remained of an attempt by Sir George to establish an oyster bed. A barrier of stones had been laid down to form a cosy little area for them. Obviously they didn't like it, and they all died.

But, back to school. Fortunately, it is in retrospect only.

That arena (I use the word advisedly) was one large room with a very small open fire place, which warmed only the teacher's backside. Large, high windows let out more heat than the fire could generate, and gave us an unrestricted view of the sky, but only of the sky, for the sills were about six feet above the floor. It would never do to let those little prisoners see the world from which they were banished every day.

That room held a conglomeration of juvenile humanity of both sexes, ranging in age from five to fourteen, at which mature age one left, to take a place in the outer world. This mob of delinquents was kept under control by one teacher, supported by a tawse, if the teacher was a female.

I liked all my female teachers, but maybe that was because they seemed to like me.   One of those delectable creatures once told me that I had the face of an angel but the nature of a devil, and maybe she was at least half right.

Our male teachers, though, were a different kettle of fish.   The last of them, under whom I suffered greatly, was friendly enough, but a helpless and lonely man during his sober periods, which were few and far between.   He was at his worst during his drying out periods, and then he was a veritable fiend.   He would appear in school, wearing big tacketty boots and knickerbockers, which helped to minimise his already diminutive stature.   He was mostly shirtless, and in place of that he wore a 'dickie'.

That dickie was once white, but was now smeared with the debris of many meals.   Prominent among them was brose, interspersed with splotches of blood, from his attempts to shave with an open razor.   That razor was called a 'cut throat', and we often wished that it lived up to its name.

He would pick up the pointer, a hard wooden rod about three feet long and an inch thick, and peer at us through blood-shot piggy eyes, and his large nose seemed to be a-quiver with venom.

He would approach his victims as if they were the demons that were burning his demented brain.   Having terrified the pupils into a state bordering on stuttering lunacy, he would select his favourite victims from among the dunderheads and dunces.   I was among the leaders in that mob.   I can still see him, approaching me with an evil grimace, crooking his finger and snarling, in his Aberdeen accent, 'Come in aboot, Erchie, come in aboot!'

That was when I was able to retreat into a hard protective shell.

In that state my mind and brain were completely immobilised and blank, and I was unable to answer any question, however simple.   But even right answers to his questions were of no help, for it was a victim he wanted, not right answers.

I was also unable to feel any pain, but have been furiously

assaulted, bounced off the desks, and beaten with the pointer, and hurled back into my seat, my collar and jacket torn, and with blue lumps, the size of pigeon eggs on the backs of my hands.

The ring-master would then collapse into his seat, his mouth agape, and completely exhausted from his orgasm of rage.   With the sleeve of my jacket, I would remove what I could of his spittle from my face, while he sat there, making little gasping sounds as he tried to regain his breath for a fresh assault on his next victim.   That was usually Angus who was on a par with me in what the master thought was the dunderhead stakes, but poor Angus was almost totally illiterate, having his head filled with knowledge of internal combustion engines.

It is surprising that we were not seriously injured by those assaults, and perhaps we were, mentally if not physically.   Certainly, although I am fairly proficient with figures, I have difficulty in adding two and two together if anyone is watching.

It was a very painful period of my life, and I find it unpleasant to recall.   The batterings I got — and they were real batterings — were not for misbehaviour, but for being what that master thought was stupid.   If I was indeed stupid, then that was how I was born, and the batterings did not help me, although perhaps they helped him in some strange way.   I realise now that he was really working out all his frustrations, miseries and failures on me and on his other victims, but the man was a brute, quite unfitted to be a schoolteacher.

Now, so many years later, I bear no bitterness for the batterings he inflicted, and I understand something of the conditions under which the unfortunate man was working.   If he had had anyone to live with and help him, his life might have been different, but he lived alone, his only companions his faithful wee Shelty collie and his addiction.   I have often wondered what his end was, the poor, helpless, misunderstood man.   Academically I believe he was a genius, and might have done so much if there had been someone to give him a bit of sympathy and understanding of his grim condition.   Instead of that, he was banished to an island, there to battle alone against his endless craving. A super-man could not have survived under those circumstances, and Peter was no super-man.

He would come to our house in the evenings to tutor my sister, and while busy doing that, his beady eyes would be glancing furtively round, watching my mother's movements, to see if she was going near the cupboard where the whisky bottle was kept. My mother, aware of the glances and the tension, would eventually say to my father, in Gaelic 'Will I give him a drop?' My father could enjoy a drop himself, and was perhaps aware of how the man was suffering, and would give her a nod of assent. After that, the tuition was more spirited, and he would launch into any subject, from the language of Chaucer to modern politics. I remember one occasion when he stretched himself back in his chair and gave my father a long lecture on, of all things, the life of the body louse! Peter's 'little drop' would allay his craving for an hour or two, but I cannot help thinking of the lonely misery he must have suffered often.

We never complained to our parents about those batterings in the school room, and passed off the torn clothing and the bruises as the hazards of the playground. Anyway, it is questionable if we would have got much sympathy from our parents. They had both received only a very elementary education, and would probably have accepted those pains as the price of modern education. Besides, in those days, the teacher was held in high esteem, not exactly gentry, perhaps, but certainly a superior being, and one whose doings were not to be questioned.

If I had any ability at school, it was in what was called 'composition', and my stories, even when I was very young, were often read out in class.

I over-reached myself one day, however.

The teacher at that time was the prim little Miss Mcnab, and she had asked us to write a story, on any subject. When this had been done, she gathered them all in and sat down behind her desk to read them. She worked through them, laying each one aside without comment, when, as we watched her, a strange look came over her previously composed expression. Her face wrinkled into a sort of strained smile, then she put her handkerchief to her mouth, rose quickly, and left the room.

I realised that it must have been my effort that had upset her composure, and now she had rushed out to let her sister, who lived with her in the school house, read it.

She was back to normal when she returned, and did not even mention compositions. I do know that it got all round the village, because on the following day my father made some veiled enquiries about the stories we wrote for our teacher.

There was no secret about it, and the story I wrote I had picked up while listening to the talk in the smiddy, where the men gathered on wet days and regaled each other with their experiences in many places and the characters they had met. Some of those men had travelled widely before coming to the island, and could be relied on for some interesting and entertaining yarns, and I wish that I had remembered all I heard, and learned, there.

The story I heard, and repeated in my composition, was told by a man who had been a drover, and it was about how he and two companions were having difficulty in persuading an obstreperous bull to go to market. They were having a hard time of it, being pulled and butted, but making little progress in the desired direction.

There was a little tinker laddie by the roadside, and he seemed to be getting a lot of pleasure from the scene, and asked them if they needed assistance. The experienced drovers thought this a bit of a joke, but as they were getting nowhere, they said they would be glad even of his assistance.

The wee laddie, carrying a stout cord in his hand, approached the rodeo, and asked the drovers if they could hold the bull still for a moment. That was about all they could do, and the tinker laddie went up quietly behind the bull and quickly looped the cord round the animal's bag and pulled it tight. According to the ex-drover the bull immediately quietened down and gave no more trouble.

I had often wondered what the bull's reaction was when the cord was removed and he had regained his 'bullhood'. Did he roar and stampede round the market, in search of the low character who had perpetrated such a dastardly deed on his regal person?

It was that story, and my thoughts about it, that shook Miss Mcnab's composure, but it earned me neither praise nor censure. The results of the exercise were never given out, but I have no doubt that the bull and bag story would find its place in the teachers' book of howlers.

No, they were certainly not happy days under the male teachers, but we did have our brighter moments with some of the women. Miss Forgan, for example, was a real darling.

Of course, she administered the strap sometimes, but she was almost in tears when she did. At home-time she would keep back whoever had been punished and take him (sometimes it was a 'her') up to her cottage, where she handed out a big slab of homemade tablet, with, sometimes, a kiss on the cheek.

Miss Forgan invariably started off the school day by holding up some newspaper and explaining to us some of the pictures there. She also read out some of the articles, and explained what they were about. Of course, with a few cunning questions, this would occupy quite a large slice of the morning, which suited us nicely. If she had no newspaper, or if there was nothing in it suitable for our delicate ears, she would instruct us in recitation and poetry reading. She herself would start off, to show us how it should be done. Her favourite was *The Battle of the Baltic*, and that would be followed by *The Eve of Waterloo*. Into those two pieces in particular she would throw all the action, drama and excitement of which she was capable, and she was capable of plenty! With froth flecking her cheeks, she held us spellbound. She was not merely reciting, she was actually there, in the midst of the battle, screaming out orders and directions to her forces, parrying and thrusting with an imaginary sword, as she stamped about the school room floor.

When the battle was over, she would sink into her seat, panting and flushed from her vivid performance.

We also would be moved by the spectacle, and when the smoke and din of battle had died away, we found it difficult to get down to dealing with the more mundane matters of education. Her recitals were not restricted to school hours, either. She lived alone, and often, from a quarter of a mile away, *The Battle of the Baltic* could be heard ringing out from her little cottage on the hillside.

Miss Forgan was a gentlewoman, in the best sense of the word. She had suffered some financial disaster, and had taken to teaching when she was no longer just a young girl. She retired to Garelochhead, and the last news I had of her was that, at over seventy years of age, she had been seen on the moor gathering sphagnum moss for the military hospitals. And that was so typical of her.

Despite all the trials and the tribulations of being educated in that little school, with twenty other pupils, we somehow almost miraculously progressed, and in the case of a few, attained high positions in their chosen pursuits. It is odd, now, looking back over so many years, to think again of those who tried to prepare us for adult life, but who were themselves such failures. They were unable to cope with their lives, and only their sad examples served to warn us against the pitfalls into which they had themselves fallen.

CHILDISH GAMES

It was a wonderful feeling to rush out of school at four o'clock, laughing and shouting with joy and relief at coming through another ordeal.

We were now at liberty to carry on with our own chosen pastimes and indulge in whatever devilry presented itself.

One of our friendly competitions was stone throwing, and it was one that could rapidly become a bit unfriendly. Neill and I were invariably top at this. Distance was the object, but to this I added accuracy, which, on occasion, I was able to put to evil purpose.

When we were not competing in a friendly way, we were trying to stone each other to death. Great stone fights took place, and as the roads were made of broken stones, there was plenty of ammunition to hand, or, rather, to foot.

In retrospect, it now amazes me that with so many showers of stones flying through the air, no one was killed or even seriously injured. What also amazes me is how we were were able to jink about, to dodge the stones as they came whizzing through the air. It was really quite thrilling, and nobody was injured, so far as I recall, when a group of us were involved. The only injuries I remember were in single combat. I had a magnificent strike one day. Angie, son of Angie of the nailed harness, had made some insulting remark to me, then hightailed it for home. He had reached the door to his house, and assuming that he was then in unassailable sanctuary, turned round and jeered about the accuracy of the stones I had been sending round his ears as he fled. I picked up a nice wee stone, just big and heavy enough to suit properly, and sent it after him.

There was no jeering about the accuracy of that one, for it knocked out two of his front teeth.   Strangely enough, I do not recall any recriminations or punishments for that: perhaps his parents accepted that it was a case of Angie's teeth or mine.

Some days later, though, my accuracy had a dramatic and startling effect on me.   I was helping to drive the cows into the byre at milking time, and was plagued by a cow that wanted to go its own way, and that was not into the byre.   There was a nice wee pebble near at hand, and I flung it with some force, enough to give the animal a good sting.   The stone was not big enough to harm the cow, but by some freak of fate, it struck right on the tip of the horn, and the animal went down as if it had been shot.   I stood, mouth agape, and gazed at it as the cow lay on its side without a quiver.   I was truly horror-struck at the thought of having killed a cow, and for about half a minute I just stood there, my mind whizzing, wondering what to do.   It was a difficult situation.   If I was found standing over a dead cow there was nothing I could think of to explain it away, expert as I was in devising explanations for difficult situations.   Just as I began to hear the rumbling of the tumbril in the distance, the cow slowly rolled over and got to its feet.   She seemed a bit groggy, but she had certainly got the messsage I had been trying to convey, and she went off quietly to the byre.   Although I had many another successful strike, that was the only 'big game' I ever brought down, and I may say that I never again threw a stone at a cow.

Some of my other strikes, although not so alarming, were sensational enough in their own way.

The hens, and especially the big Rhode Island cock, were fair game, I thought, particularly as they played havoc among the seeds in our garden.   The sight of them having a dust bath in a newly-sown seed bed seemed to arouse me (perhaps the killer instinct in embryo), and I would chase them furiously, pelting with stones.   The hens were nimble, and were over the fence and into the raspberry bushes in a flash.   The big fat cockerel, though, was not built for speed, and more than once he caught a stone on some part of his anatomy.   Once, I even caught him on the head, and the result, although not so alarming as with the cow, was equally dramatic. He keeled over immediately.

I thought I was justified in what I had done, but just the same appreciated that it was serious. Killing the father of the flock would not be taken lightly. I watched anxiously as he got to his feet, and then gyrated slowly with his head on one side. He continued circling for a while, with his head pointing the wrong way, and then, much to my relief, and no doubt to his relief, too, his beak began to point in the right direction. He stood still for a moment, took one last giddy look around, and slowly ambled off.

But there was a sequel to this. I had not known it, but my mother had seen the cockerel's strange gyrations, but not the cause of it. She was convinced that he was past his prime and suffering from dizziness. So my father pulled his neck, and I must say that he looked a lot better on the table than he had going round in circles, looking over his shoulder.

There were many other occupations than stoning the hens during the summer holidays, and the most soul-destroying was winkle gathering. Certainly it was remunerative, but how we hated it!

Our mothers were constantly engaged in that task, and it was a backbreaker. Even outwith the holidays, we were expected to join them, if the tide was right, as soon as we returned from school, and on those days we were as reluctant to get home as we had been to get to school. It is astonishing how many diversions a small boy can find on any errand, if he really tries. Never was a tide so slow to turn and flood the shore as on those days when we were busy at the winkles. It seemed to go out and then stand still for hours. Finger nails we had none: they were worn down almost to the knuckles. Picking winkles would be the perfect cure for nail-biters: there would be nothing left to bite!

The winkles we gathered so painfully were put in sacks and stored below high water mark, where the tide washed over them twice a day, and kept them fresh. When enough had been collected, they were all sorted out and cleaned (almost shampooed, it seemed to me), then re-bagged and sent off to Billingsgate in distant London, courtesy of Mr. MacBrayne and his wonderful steamers. Every bag we sent off carried our special coded wooden tag, and eventually that tag would be returned, with payment for the fish. It was never very much, and seemed ridiculously small when I thought of the time and energy and pain involved, but beyond doubt it meant something in the very tight economy of that household. I seem to remember that the best price we ever received for our winkles was eight shillings and six pence (forty-two new pence) for a bushel, and there are a hell of a lot of winkles to a bushel, and every winkle had been individually picked, bagged, washed, re-bagged and cherished, at a cost of frozen hands and feet and backs bent for hours on a wind-spent beach.

We did have our illnesses, of course, but few of them serious enough to keep us off the winkles. The complaints considered serious enough to do that were usually measles, whooping cough and 'flu, all contributions from the mainland, brought by visitors.

My sister brought the whooping cough from Oban, and of the seven children in the family, I was the only one who escaped the infection. There was one standard treatment for at least the initial stages of all childish ailments, and that was castor oil. The equally dreaded 'Jallap' was kept for routine use, not for illness.

We were all reluctant to admit to illness of any sort, knowing what was in store for us. Inevitably, though, the patient would be bundled up the stairs and into bed, to lie there and listen to the vile brew being prepared down below. I almost imagine I hear it still, that rapid clicking as the potion was mixed up with a fork in a bowl. That was the castor oil, being switched into a ghastly froth with hot milk. It was rushed quickly up the stairs to reach the victim before the oil had again floated to the top. What a mixture to look into when you were already feeling sick!

The co-operation of the patient could not be counted on, and a scrimmage usually followed. But somehow it seemed that the forces of law always had some assistance to call on, and somehow that assistance always seemed to be an elderly aunt, a sister of my mother, who often stayed with us. She would be called on to supply the extra muscle, and aunts are still one of my great aversions.

The aunt always seemed to enjoy her part of the operation, sadistically nipping the patient's nose with a determined grip of forefinger and thumb until the victim was forced to surface for breath. Immediately there was a gap, the contents of the bowl were sloshed into it, or round about it, before the gap disappeared again. It was all a difficult and confusing operation, with first one side and then the other winning. Before the stramash had subsided, there was usually as much of the filthy mess on the outside of the patient as inside. But the result was never really in doubt: the patient went to pot!

There were other so-called cures, equally crude and drastic, although perhaps not so traumatic. One of these was carried out by a qualified doctor.

That doctor lived on the island of Eigg, and rarely stirred from there, although he was officially the doctor for all the Small Isles. If he was needed on Rhum, he was called by the telephone circuit, but it had to be a desperate need, and even then there was no certainty that he could get to the island across the Sound. Often enough, he arrived after a gale had blown itself out, to find that his services were no longer needed, the patient having responded to the gentle administrations of the local experts — and everyone was an expert with medicine. Sometimes the call for the doctor would be cancelled, again using that new-fangled telephone, and that suited everybody.

Fortunately, though, the doctor had relatives on Rhum, and on rare occasions he would choose a pleasant summer day to make a semi-official visit. He was a big man, with an enormous paunch which appeared to have been specially moulded to support the gold chain that adorned the imposing mound, a mound which he carried with great dignity.

On one of those visits, after he had belched his way through a good meal (we got all the details of this from the children of the house where he had dined) he was asked to call on Mrs. MacLean, to attend to some sort of growth on the back of her hand.   He examined it, and then called for boiling water, into which he dipped a pair of borrowed scissors.   He then smartly snipped off the growth, slapped on a plaster and was away home to his whisky before the poor woman had a chance to realise what was happening.

It happened that I was an interested observer of that operation on Mrs. MacLean, and was fascinated by the whole procedure.   But I was thankful that I had nothing that needed similar treatment.   It was all over in seconds, though, and in that at least it compared very favorably with the dreaded castor oil treatment.

We had all kinds of patent medicines to treat simple ailments, such as 'Cooling Powders' for every kind of fever.   I have no idea whether they worked, but every house had a stock of them, and if the supply ran out in the patient's house, then there were other houses to scurry to for a replenishment.   We never seemed to be completely stuck for the magic, fever-reducing powder.   Everybody had faith in those powders, and perhaps that was enough to produce the desired result.

Any chesty wheezing was treated with 'Camphorated Oil', well massaged into the chest.   It was a horrible proceeding, and the effectiveness of the treatment seemed to be measured by the amount of pressure applied during the application.   The unfortunate sufferer would splutter and gasp as the strong fumes rose up and the oily hand clattered and bumped over the bones of the chest and shoulders.   The fumes of the freshly applied oil were really quite nauseating and irritating, and seemed to make the treatment worse than the complaint. When both patient and nurse were in a lather of sweat from the treatment, the whole area was covered with part of a woolly blanket, which had to be worn continuously until the wheezing disappeared. This could easily run into weeks, and the oil continued to give off its fumes for all that time.   It created an aura of rejection, both in school and out, which had to be accepted as part of the cure.   I suppose that the almost intolerable itching from the woolly blanket was also part of the cure, but at least that could be relieved by a good scratch, while the smell went on all the time.

Wounds required different, and sometimes more urgent, treatment.

My young brother was playing on the shore one day and had the end of his big toe cut off by a piece of glass. He was a heavy lad, but I lifted him and took off for home like a long dog, the blood from his injured toe running down my trouser leg. When I dropped the burden on the floor, I was in a state of collapse, but nobody had any time for me in the ensuing commotion and uproar. Orders and instructions were shouted and countermanded, armchairs were over-turned and dingy corners searched for cobwebs. None could be found, and as my mother held a rag over the still bleeding toe she sent me scurrying next door to resume the search.

Mrs. MacGillivray (Red Maggie, as she was called), was resting, as usual, when I burst in, still panting from my run with the injured lad. Maggie, who was never guilty of making sudden or energetic movements, did something she had never been known to do before. She leaped into action and, in a flash, (which for Maggie was a quick amble), was down on her knees in front of the sink in the scullery.

There was a large expanse of grey-bloomered backside as she dived deep into the abyss. You could see and hear intense activity as she dived deeper, like a badger clearing out an old sett. Old boxes, pots, pans and pails, all were thrown out behind her and rattled along the concrete floor until at least she reversed out, holding aloft, trium-phantly, a large spider's web, to which adhered the accumulated debris of years. There were the shrivelled bodies of bluebottles, long since sucked dry, together with the discarded skins of the spiders which had sucked them dry. Goodness knows how long they had carried on their relentless slaughter in that dark recess, completely unaware that the result of all their efforts, as they spun and slew down beneath the sink, would one day be so urgently sought.

This whole thing, dry bluebottles, old spiders, butterfly wings and a good mixing of plain muck, was rushed through to my mother with all the speed of a donor's kidney, and handed to her as if it was the Holy Grail itself. She snatched it, and slapped it on to the bleeding toe,

101

and wrapped it securely round.   The bleeding stopped immediately, and, with a sigh of relief, my mother picked off the most accessible of the bluebottles and other extraneous bits.   In all fairness, I should say that the underside of the web, which went onto the wound, did seem cleaner than the outside.

After the turmoil and the tension had eased off, my mother and Maggie settled down for a cup of tea, while Donnie was released, to walk on his heel for a few days.   I experienced that sort of thing myself, and know that after the wound has healed, it is quite difficult to get into the normal stride again.

Minor ailments, some of them painful, were dealt with in various and curious ways.

For toothache, the accepted treatment was the insertion of a clove into the aching cavity, or a bit of cotton wool soaked in whisky placed between the gum and cheek.   I don't suppose that either of them cured the toothache, but the burning sensation of the clove or whisky certainly helped to overcome the pain for a short time.

Earache was dealt with by heating an onion, and plonking it as hot as bearable over the ear.   This did not, I know, do much good, because the pain returned as the onion cooled, but if it gave at least temporary relief, it was worthwhile.   Anyway, the onion could always be used for tomorrow's stew.

For some reason, treatment of the common cold was usually left to the discretion of the sufferer, with no standard remedies for it.   Consequently, the treatments came in various and weird forms.   One of my own served at least at well as the others, and I was not allowed to forget it.   This happened on the night before our weekly dance, and was, for me, one of those little tragedies that seem to mark childhood and growing up.   I had developed a sore throat, with all the symptoms of an impending heavy cold, and retired early to bed.

When my mother came up the stairs, she was astounded to find me in full fighting rig.   My own cure for the sore throat was a sock, securely fastened round the neck, but it was no ordinary sock; it was a well-used and fully ripe one.   The ripeness was, apparently, required for my treatment. A clean one would have been lacking in potency. Probably I had picked up this idea from listening around in the smithy, where I often heard things that were not meant for the likes of me. I was submerged in the blankets, and, with the curative sock round my neck, all that was visible was my nose sticking out below a big tea cosy I had rammed on my head. However, the treatment seemed to be effective, because I was at the dance the following night, in my sister's discarded high-heeled shoes.

Spring and autumn were marked in our household by the ceremony of Sulphur and Treacle, that awful alleged cleanser and tonic. Somehow, it all seemed to be mixed with religion and missionaries, for we had learned that sulphur was that same brimstone with which the Devil threatened us. Whether we were good or bad, though, twice a year we underwent the cleansing ceremony. It was filthy stuff, and had to be almost forced down us. Another strike against all aunts, for it seemed there was always one of those there to help in administering the dose.

Even my father under strong protest, was coerced into taking his dose of the allegedly blood-purifying mixture. He always had the first dollop, to show what a brave lad he was and to encourage the younger fry. My mother firmly believed in the stuff, but he was a non-believer. One day, though, he was finally converted, and even we children were impressed, when, after a liberal dose, my mother told him to take off his socks and shake them over the fire. To our astonishment, yellow dust came out of the socks, and blue flames spread over the burning coals. We were all convinced that his whole system was being cleaned out of whatever it was supposed to be cleansed of. Thereafter, his gab was the first to be opened, and that willingly, when we lined up each night for a week each spring and autumn. It was several years later that I realised my mother had played a trick on him and on us, and had liberally sprinkled his socks with Flowers of Sulphur. I don't suppose that the noxious mixture had any effect on us, good or bad, but our general good health was always attributed to it. It was fortunate that all the children in the school were similarly treated, and at about the same time, because one result of the dosing was a great increase in flatulence, and the results of that flatulence were unmistakeable. We all suffered, and no-one could be blamed.

STAGS AND SHEEP

Stone throwing seems to have played a biggish part in my childhood, and there were at least three times when I regretted it, and still regret it. The first was when I knocked out Angie's front teeth, but somehow that seemed to be more in the nature of natural justice, and although I still have the occasional twinge of conscience about it, it does not unduly disturb me.

The wee black and white terrier dog is different. He was having a great time, enjoying himself immensely, jumping about in the long grass and weeds, searching for mice. What a treat he was having, and what a change for him, for he spent most of his life on a fishing boat, and had just been brought ashore for his Sunday run. At that time there were no other dogs on the island, except those of the shepherds and gamekeepers: they were forbidden to us.

So a strange terrier was a different matter. It was not one of us, and therefore, it seemed, was fair game. I hit him on the shoulder with a fair sized stone, thrown with my usual accuracy, and he whimpered and limped off on three legs. The fisherman must have known it was no accident, but I had no punishment for my crime, just a bad conscience for the next seventy-five years, and no chance to make amends or apologise to the wee dog.

Another time I killed a cock chaffinch stone dead, literally. That picture, too, has lingered on through the years, and I can still see it lying dead, with its lovely wings and slender legs trembling.

Ronnie and I had been on a rat safari when we saw the bird sitting on a beam of wood in the sunshine. The hunting instinct was uppermost, but I had no intention of killing or even hurting the bird. However, I killed it with the first shot. Ronnie and I were both fond of birds, and looked at the body with dismay. Ultimately, we settled on a solution

105

that was almost Jesuitical. We decided that the bird, seeing the stone approaching, had skipped smartly to one side and struck its head on a protruding nail. We concluded it had died from miscalculation and misadventure.

I don't know what was really in Ronnie's mind at the time, but in mine there was a numb and niggling conviction that I had without doubt killed the little thing. Those two incidents, of the dog and the bird, have stuck with me throughout a long life, and still give me twinges now and again.

The seven children in our family arrived in quick succession, and we slept more or less where we could, in the beds upstairs. There were no particular places: those who got to bed first got the best positions. The last got the outside place, up against the outside wall of the house. On a stormy night, you could actually feel the wall being pushed in, and those were solidly built cottages, not rough shanties.

The storms did not worry me, but the corncrakes did. We never heard those infernal birds during the day, but during the quiet summer evenings, when every other creature, including us, wanted to get to sleep, they would waken up and have a conversation with their friends, or else challenge every enemy for miles around.

They were interesting birds, though, but most frustrating, as we discovered when we tried to find them. They seem to have some sort of ventriloquist ability, and are never where they seem to be. Years later, after I had left the island, and had returned on a holiday, I enquired after the corncrakes, and was told that certainly some had hatched, but that the 'mudges' had killed them all! It doesn't seem very likely, but anyone knowing the midges of Rhum would not dismiss the story lightly.

When the corncrake season was over, the stags began their celebrations, which were much more aggressive than anything the birds could do.

It was the rutting, or mating, season, and all hell broke loose. At times, they would surround our house and make the very air quiver with their roaring.

On one particularly wild night we hardly got any sleep at all. There seemed to be two opposing herds, one gang being in the garden and the other just over the fence, and they fought all night. We knew we were safe, but it was fearsome to listen to their roars and the clashing of antlers, which went on all night. When we inspected the battleground next morning, the destruction was indescribable, with the ground all torn up and the garden fence scattered over a wide area. My mother and I had a narrow escape. We had been along the hillside gathering brambles, and arrived home just at dusk. As we reached home, we could already hear the roars of the stags as they converged on their chosen battle field, which happened to be our garden.

Game keepers and other pundits say that a stag will not attack a man. Under normal circumstances that may be true, but an enraged stag, roused to battle fury by challenges and taunts from his opponents, will attack anything. I have seen one viciously attacking a telegraph pole when there was nothing else available.

Tame stags, having lost their fear of man, can be very dangerous. There was one, befriended by Miss Forgan, the teacher. She lived alone, as did most of our teachers, and they all seemed to be constantly on the lookout for a bit of diversion to lighten their lonely existence. One found her diversion in the heather with a sailor, and had to leave in a hurry. Miss Forgan found a stag, and diverted to it a lot of love and affection, the sort of thing that would have made any sailor very happy.

The teacher's cottage bordered on the moor, and Miss Forgan made a habit of feeding the deer over the boundary fence. One stag became so tame that it would take bread from her hand. She called him 'Copey', and often told us in school about his friendliness and intelligence. She always carried a bit of bread in her pocket when out walking in case she met her friend on the road, and of course this pleased 'Copey' who would go on his way, on the look out for other

107

walkers, who might be equally generous.

One day Copey met a sailor from the *Rhouma*, and came boldly forward to demand his bread, but of course sailors do not normally carry bread in their pockets. Copey did not know this, and tried a few snorts and pushes and nudges. When he realised that there was to be no handout, he attacked the sailor viciously. Fortunately, it was in the early part of the year, when the stag had cast his antlers, but just the same a stag can inflict severe damage with his hooves, which are very sharp. The unfortunate sailor was knocked to the ground and set upon by the now enraged stag, and suffered quite severe injuries. Copey was shot after that, and Miss Forgan censured for having turned a wild animal into a 'tame' one.

Birds and animals, in their season, provided us with diversion and entertainment, but the best was the sheep clipping. Once a year, all the sheep were herded in from their various hirsels of Kilmory, Harris, Guridale and Dibidale to Kinloch, where the fanks, shearing sheds and dipping tanks were situated.

This was a very busy time, and noisy with the bleating of sheep, the barking of dogs and the whistling and shouting of the shepherds as they drove in their various flocks to the allocated pens in the fank, to be sorted out, dipped or clipped and stamped with their hirsel number.

The lambs would be separated from their mothers and driven into a field by themselves, there to keep up a constant wailing all night long, one which rang in our ears for days after they had been taken away and permanently parted from their mothers.

On our way to school, we had to force our way through this great mass of sheep, dogs and shepherds, to fidget through the rest of the day until we were finally released to take part in what was still left of the operation. School bags cast aside, we would dive into the fray.

The clipping would be well advanced by the time we were released from our scholastic purgatory for the day. The long, pear-shaped clipping stools were set in rows, and the animal being clipped was placed, with two legs tethered, on the wide end of the stool while the clipper made himself comfortable, straddle-legged, at the other.

There was no mechanisation about the job, of course, and the clippers worked with hand shears, which they provided themselves, and which they looked after with the greatest care. They were literally as sharp as razors, and when not in use were kept carefully in oil-soaked leather scabbards. Every shepherd prided himself on the condition of his shears, and indeed his reputation amongst his fellows depended on it.

We lads appointed ourselves as 'croggers'. It was our task to collect the sheep from the pens and deliver them to the clippers, and, above all, not to keep any of the clippers waiting.

Now, crogging was an easy enough job when the pens were full and the sheep could not move around much. By the time we got there, the pens were emptying, and each sheep had to be chased and caught. These were sheep off the moors, wild and scared. They had never been handled by man since the last clipping, indeed, had scarcely even seen a human being except in the distance. They were not easy to catch and hold. But we were there for a bit of excitement, and we got plenty of that, with some rough treatment and trampled feet into the bargain.

The ground in the fanks was made of rough granite chippings, and in a short time it was mixed into a horrible mess of sheep dung and grit. Very sore it was on the bare feet, and that was without the added pain of being trampled on by the sharp 'clits' of the animals. If you tried it yourself, you might wonder why we did it, and even more, why we enjoyed it all!

Some of the animals were big tough beasts, and the only way for us to handle them was to mount them and guide them into the clipping shed by their horns. They did not take kindly to this, and would bolt madly round the fank, cracking our toes and legs against the railings. Quite often, only the timely opening of the gate would save the rider, clinging desperately to his mount, from being trampled into the muck. The rodeo would end with a mad gallop in among the clipping stools until, thankfully, someone bigger would take a hand and subdue the frightened animal.

109

After they were clipped, the sheep were marked with their hirsel number by means of an an iron stencil dipped into hot tar. There was always a good deal of competition between the clippers to be the first to shout 'Tar!'. One shepherd, who was a notoriously slow worker with the shears, doing about one beast to everyone else's three, would shout out, very loudly 'Tar AGAIN!' His call was always greeted with derision from the rest of the gang, but it didn't trouble him in the least. He had clipped his sheep and was entitled to his stamp like the rest of them.

The marker's job was an easy one. All he had to do was keep the tar hot and the marking iron poised, ready to dip it and run before the animal was released. We often envied the chap who got that job, but the post was always filled long before we arrived. By contrast, our task of galloping about among stone chips and sheep dung, getting our bare feet torn by sharp hooves, must have given the impression that we were tough, dedicated, or perhaps mad, especially as we got nothing out of it except satisfaction. But, man, it was sore on the feet!

We were also learning other things than how to catch sheep.

The back chat and laughter-creating jokes bandied about among the shearers was crude and often lurid. It was all in Gaelic, of course, and I believe the men were under the impression that most of their remarks were over our heads. We were not supposed to know much about the facts of life, certainly not enough to follow their ribaldry. But they were wrong!

Sexy and outspoken most of the conversation was, and indeed sometimes unintelligible to us, but here and there our sharp ears would detect a familiar word, or even a whole sentence, which when fitted together gave us most of the story, and also the reason for a lot of the laughter that rang out.

One shepherd, Sandy Nicholson, from a remote hirsel, was the butt of much of the ribaldry. In an unguarded moment, Sandy had announced that the night before his wife had given birth to a son. It was an event for jubilation as far as Sandy was concerned, and should have been, he thought, equally so for his companions.

But their glee was on a different plane from Sandy's, as he soon found out. They pounced on the poor man, quite mercilessly, and the stream of comments and questions about the event and the circumstances came at him all day as some new angle presented itself to the more nimble minded or cruder characters. Sandy's glee had turned to gall by the end of the day.

Apart from being the father, Sandy had also been the midwife, as his nearest neighbour was seven miles away. This was grist to the mill, and another boon to his tormentors. They bombarded him with quips, queries and suggestions of possible action he should have taken, from pre-conception to the birth. One of the suggestions was that he should have put a *moccan* on it. A *moccan* is a half sock, worn instead of slippers, and our active minds immediately latched onto the word, and we realised what was meant, as a half sock would not serve any useful purpose except to keep the feet warm, and Sandy's feet were not being discussed, although just about every other part of his anatomy was.

At the best of times, Sandy was not very articulate. Perhaps the big moustache that shrouded his mouth had something to do with that, but it would have taken more than the removal of that obstacle to enable Sandy to cope with the bombardment that assailed him that day.

We croggers, with typical juvenile suspicion and perception, realised from the uproar of laughter that there was more to all this than immediately met our ears, and, while not neglecting our duties, lingered in the clipping shed as long as possible. We picked up many tit-bits that way, which we digested and later compared with the gleanings of our fellow croggers. A lot of interesting information was assimilated that way, and, piecing it together, we learned quite a lot about Sandy's mismanagement of his marital affairs, what he had done, what he had failed to do, what he should have done, and the consequences of whatever it was he had done.

After the clipping came the dipping, a messy and dirty business, in which there was no time and no inclination for banter and merriment,

111

everyone being intent on getting the operation over as soon as possible. We erstwhile croggers viewed this from a distance, perched on the top of the railings above the tank, to avoid the showers of dip thrown up as the sheep were pushed into the nauseous mixture.

The actual dipper, clad in oilskins and sou'wester, stood beside the tank and grabbed the sheep as they were thrown into the stinking liquid. ' Holding the animal by the back of the neck, he would push it deep into the mixture, collecting almost as much tick-and-scab killer as the animals themselves. Everyone was greatly relieved when that dirty job was finished.

The shepherds, each with his own flock, would then slowly and gladly wend their way home to their own peaceful and uncomplicated existence on their own little patches with their own wives and children.

We children enjoyed an occasional visit to those outposts, where we were invariably well fed on home baked scones and butter milk, but we saw little of the children who lived there. They were very shy, and hid when strangers approached, and stayed hidden until the strangers left.

One story about our own family went around the clipping shed, and caused a lot of laughter, although it had nothing at all to do with the sort of problems besetting poor Sandy.

Most of our home entertainment was provided by my father. In many ways he was strict and in others rather lax, even indulgent. One thing he was strict about was good table manners and proper behaviour at meal times. All meals were preceded by a very solemn Grace, and no food was eaten until that ritual had been performed. At one particular meal, porridge had been served, and as it cooled on the plates, a tough skin formed on top. We seven youngsters were sitting around the table, waiting for the head of the house to give the signal to dive in.

For some reason he was late in appearing, and to break the boredom, one adventurous spirit discovered that the contents of the plates were solid enough to be turned out and balanced on the palm of the hand. When my mother made porridge, she made real solid stuff. Anyway, that enterprising lad had started something which challenged the rest of us, and in a moment we were all involved in the performance, some less successfully than others.

My brother Iain was unfortunate in that he had made a beautiful turnover and was displaying it triumphantly when my father appeared. The exhibition of disregard for the sanctity of the not-yet-blessed food was too much for him. His shout upset Iain's sense of balance and the pat of solidified porridge fell to the floor with a resounding flop. This really put the 'cat amang the doos', and my father reacted quickly. In his rush to get at the culprit and deliver the usual manual reprimand, he failed to see the pat on the floor, put his stockinged foot in it, and went Scoosh! the length of the room on his backside. Iain escaped that time, and escaped eating the porridge, too, for it was liberally smeared over the floor and over the posterior of his father. In fact, he got nothing, for the pot was empty, but that would not have troubled him: he didn't much like porridge anyway, and quite possibly had been raiding the feeding shed in the farm yard.

We raided the feeding shed at every opportunity, and must have been a thorn in the flesh — several thorns in fact — to all the farm managers. If the door of the shed was left open and unguarded for a moment, we were in like a gang of street Arabs. There was a barrel of treacle there, with a handy tap. We would turn on the tap and lap up the treacle from our hands. More than once, that tap was left open, and the treacle running over the floor, when we scooted out on the approach of authority. It was enough to rouse fury in any farm manager, however easy-going.

Perhaps because it was a forbidden fruit, we really enjoyed that treacle, but not so at home. Apart from its association with the gruesome brimstone and treacle medication, we were sometimes faced with the stuff at breakfast time, poured over our porridge. That was when, owing to misfortune or mismanagement, the cows would be dry, and the resulting drought meant there was no milk for porridge.

113

During those periodical droughts, syrup or treacle would be poured over the porridge. Syrup was acceptable, just, but treacle, never! It all had to be eaten, though, under the strict supervision of my mother, who hovered around to make sure that all plates were emptied. They were, too, although we usually left the table ganting at the last spoonful. Iain learned the trick of packing quite a lot of the hateful stuff into the sides of his cheeks, and would then spout it out to the hens at the back door. They did not seem to share our prejudices about it.

To our regret, there was no syrup kept in the feeding shed. We liked the stuff, and would dive a spoon into the tin whenever we got the chance.

Another delicacy kept in the feeding shed was locust beans. You never see these today, but we thought them grand eating. I never discovered where they are grown, but later, on the mainland, I found that you could buy them in sweetie shops at four for a halfpenny, and often appeased my longing for sweet things with them, walking down the street, chewing away at the long brown pods.

At the farm, they were chopped up and mixed with the rest of the animal feed, and to get at them we had to dive into the deep bin and scrabble amongst the mixture. Several of us could be in the bin at the same time, boring and burrowing away, well aware that we could be trapped at any moment. That happened more than once, and the first we knew of it would be the banging of the heavy lid down over our heads and the snap of the latch. We would be left there to stew for a while, thinking about the risks involved in our locust mining, until whoever it was who had caught us would relent and open the lid. We would emerge, covered in dust and panting for air, to get a clout on the ear as we rushed out of the shed.

There were some real bonanzas, though, when we found the key in the shed door and the men all away in the hayfields. Then we could really clean up. With tins filled with treacle and pockets filled with locust beans we would be off hot-foot to the nearest wood, or to the hay loft where the booty was consumed.

114

Another source of loot was the troughs where the tups were fed.   It was less risky than raiding the feeding shed, but sometimes entailed a long and frustrating wait while we watched our locusts being eaten by the tups, whose food it really was.   If the shepherd had not seen us hiding behind the hedge (and he knew perfectly.well what we were up to — he had probably done the same thing himself as a lad) he would pour the mixture into the troughs and be off at once.   We acted quickly then, to prevent the tups from gobbling up all the precious locusts.   We attacked the troughs just as greedily as the tups, but if we had been delayed by the shepherd, we were often too late.   Tups are greedy beasts, and just as fond of food as we were.   We were usually fortunate though, and salvaged a few, even if they had been slobbered over by the tups.   A quick wipe down the trouser leg sorted that out.   The rest of the mixture did not attract us.   We left that to the tups, who probably needed it more than we did.

The locusts, and whole ones at that, were fed to the deer in the winter, but we could not steal any from them.   A hungry stag was a different proposition than a well-fed tup.

I knew this from personal experience.   I looked out of the window one morning and saw a big stag eating our cabbages.   Having visions of our winter stews being thinner than usual, I rushed out, intent on driving him off.   The big fellow would have none of it.   As I approached him at a rush, he took two steps towards me and stuck out his tongue and waggled it about as stags do when they are angry.   He was annoyed at this interruption to his breakfast, and having seen angry stags in action, I had no intention of discussing the matter with this one.   I retired at a smart and undignified canter, and watched, impotently, as he leisurely finished the cabbages and jumped over the fence, with a derogatory flick of his white tail.

On a later occasion, in a burst of bravado in front of my companions, I charged barefoot, through an area of broken glass and cinders, at a stag which had laid claim to an area to which we thought we had prior rights.   The beast stood his ground until, with this blustering idiot almost on the tips of his antlers, he lost his nerve and turned tail.   Had I been alone, I would never have thought of carrying out that bit of bravado, but, having started the charge, I had to carry it through, but I wonder what I would have done had that stag stood his ground.

RATS

There was one occasion when I would have been better to have done as the stag did, and run away from my enemy.

I have already written about my ability to throw stones straight and strong, and of injuries I inflicted that way. But Nemesis was at hand. Nemesis was in fact Willie, with whom I had some sort of quarrel, and I hit him so hard with something that I knew retaliation was inevitable, and probably painful.

Willie was a strong and determined lad, and very quick tempered. When aroused, he could easily destroy me, and now I feared that he would. I knew nothing could save me but flight, and that I had the best of it there. So I was off like a startled doe round the bothy, and getting further in front of Willie with every flash of my bare feet.

I had hoped that Willie would give up the chase, but he was really determined this time, and kept on going. He might have made better speed had he not stopped to pick up a missile. This was a heavy stone big enough to fell an ox, and Willie was determined to use it on me. We went on up the field, but then I thought he had me, for there was the stone dyke to scramble over. I did get over it, though, with Willie close behind, and then I thought I was safe, safe enough to stand and jeer. Even if Willie came over the dyke, there was only the open moor in front of us, and I knew I could easily outpace him there. Jeering was a bad mistake. Willie did not even try to climb the dyke, but just launched his stone at me. Under different circumstances, and as no mean thrower of stones myself, I would have applauded his aim, for the stone sped fast and true, bounced off my head and felled me to the ground.

I am sure Willie thought he had killed me, for he was off home, at a good speed, and took refuge under the bed.

When I came to, I also made for home, but with a lump as big as a swan's egg on the top of my head. My mother examined this with some alarm, but, finally convinced I was not going to drop dead, demanded to know who was reponsible. I must have been dazed, for I told her, something which normally I would never have done. Some elaborate story of natural mishap would have been made up, not very convincing perhaps, but good enough for the moment. To give the name of any enemy like that was quite against all principles and laws of our boyhood. When she heard that Willie was responsible, she grasped me firmly by the hand and hustled me off, feet hardly touching the ground, to confront Willie's mother and demand retribution for changing the shape of my head. It had to be done quickly, before the lump lost any of its pristine beauty.

The altercation was heated, as my mother pointed to the lump and insisted that the wicked Willie be brought forward to view the result of his malicious attack on an innocent boy. Oh, the touching faith of mothers in the Christ-like character of their own off-spring!

The two women retreated to the bedroom and through the closed door I could still hear the cries of recrimination and protest as they tried to outshout each other. Eventually, after all had been said that could be said, it was decided to take action against the villain. But that was not easy, either, as the new sounds from the bedroom indicated. There was a lot of shuffling and banging of furniture, muffled squeals and cries of 'Come out of there!' But Willie was too firmly entwined round the leg of the bed to be dislodged.

All this while I was standing in the living room, with a throbbing head, under the baleful eye of a huge stuffed fish on the wall. I felt that it resented my presence there, disturbing what was otherwise a peaceful enough household. Finally, having vented sufficient ire on what was available of Willie, and having extracted fervent promises of improvement in his future behavior, the two mothers parted, amicably enough, but with a slightly stiff manner, and I was led home, to have the lump reduced by applications of cloots and cold water.   It was all just an episode in growing up, and Willie and I were soon again the best of friends, the closest of cronies, and sometimes the scourge of the village.

There was one other unpleasant memory of that period, but it concerned me alone.   Not even Willie was involved.

Years later, I had a good friend, a joiner, and a real artist at his work.   When he was busy with some particularly intricate work, he would sing a little rhyme:

A house without a roof, my friends,
A ship without a sail,
But a more uncomfortable thing, my friends,
Is a shirt without a tail.

I have no idea where the ditty came from, but I believe it was wrong.   It is a strange thing about shirts.   When I was a lad and a young man, shirts had proper tails to them, tails that could be tucked between the legs and brought up the front, like some sort of elaborate loin-cloth.   They certainly helped to keep you warm, but they had one disadvantage.   Any minor call of nature meant a good deal of fumbling around before the necessary implement came to hand, and that could cause some panic if things were pressing.   Today, shirts seem to have almost no tail at all, hardly enough to stuff into the waistband, far less to form into that comfortable and warming loin-cloth.

Anyway, I had acquired a shirt from somewhere which boasted a tail even longer than usual.   It was tremendous, a very mammoth of a tail which reached to well below my knees.

We lads, of course, like the men, slept in our shirts: there were no such cissy luxuries as pyjamas.   They would have been considered a time-consuming and unnecessary complication, even had we ever heard of such things.   The girls had their 'goonies', but we slept in our shirts.   There was no nonsense about changing to go to bed and it was straight out of bed and into the trousers, and that was us, almost fully dressed.

This particular night I was wearing my long-tailed shirt and disaster fell. For the only time I can remember, I wet the bed. None of the other occupants seemed to have noticed anything amiss, and I was careful to be last out that morning. I felt around the bed, and, praise be! it was dry. My colossal shirt-tail had justified itself. On that occasion it was not an inch too long.

It was all wet and heavy and uncomfortable as I pushed the sodden mass into my trousers. There was no alternative, I had to take it all with me or risk discovery and scorn. I rammed the horrid mess into my trousers, fastened everything down securely, ate my breakfast standing up and went off to school.

It was an uncomfortable walk, and it was uncomfortable sitting in school. Each time I moved, my bare skin encountered a new wet and chilly area. Eventually, it all warmed and dried out, and life became more bearable.

That is why I would like to change the last line of my joiner friend's jingle to: *Is a shirt with a long wet tail.*

The castle pigs provided us with some amusement, and some trouble. They had been brought in to eat the waste from the castle. They were quite young when they arrived, pink and clean in the straw of the large loose box. Young perhaps, but quite big enough for some mischief. Even before they had their first feed from the castle waste bins, we were in there with them, amongst the straw.

They seemed to be just the right size for riding, and so ride them we did, until each of our mounts collapsed. Then we chose another, and continued the furious and very noisy rodeo until the farm manager appeared, roaring even more than the pigs were squealing. He was in amongst us in a moment, and it was our turn to squeal as he booted us out. I suppose really that it was fortunate that he was nearby, otherwise we might have killed the young pigs.

I really don't know whether or not we lads were more cruel there on the island than lads elsewhere. It was not any sort of calculated cruelty, more thoughtlessness, but even so the memory of some of the things we did continues to trouble me to this day. Another episode again concerned the pigs. By this time the lovely little pink animals had flourished on their rich diet of waste food, and had grown into large, almost obscene porkers. One of the ways we tormented them was first to trap a wasp in a matchbox, then, when it popped its head out, behead the insect by snapping the matchbox shut. Not surprising, this upset the insect, and its sting began work, going in and out in great style. The headless wasp was then dropped onto the broad back of a pig, and the fun, for us, began. In a moment the soundly sleeping pig was on its feet, after the first jab, pondering the situation and with suspicious blue eyes looking around for the culprit. At the second jab, he was away round the pen, rubbing his back on all the walls, and squealing enough to be heard in Mallaig. We enjoyed this, even if the pigs and the wasps got little pleasure from it.

Another use for beheaded wasps was to drop them over the bridge, where there was a good shoal of hungry trout. The insect would no sooner touch the water than it would be snapped up and pulled down. It didn't stay down for very long, though, and in an instant was up again, to be eagerly grabbed by another unsuspecting fish. Somehow, the news soon got around that this food could bite back, and the whole shoal would sheer off. They had short memories, and within a few days could be stung again.

After seeing this, I have always distrusted those pundits who assure us that fish feel no pain. I think our experiment, which was not carried out in the interests of science, shows that they do, and that they can learn lessons.

Stags, fish, pigs, stones, lumps on the head — they were all interesting, at times painful, and all accepted as part of our growing up. This list of sports, and the creatures that provided it, would not be complete without the ubiquitous rat. They were everywhere, in their hundreds, and we pursued them with enthusiasm, and with all the death-dealing implements at our disposal.

I well remember baiting a large home-made cage trap with herring guts and setting it out in the middle of the garden. In the morning, when I looked out of the window, it appeared to be solid with the brutes. In fact, after we had drowned them, the total count was twenty-three, a good haul for one night.

Our favorite implement was the gin trap, now fortunately illegal. We set them in the runs under the fences, or in the grass, where the creatures went into the corn fields to feed. Checking our trap line in the mornings added a bit of spice to getting out of bed. Unfortunately, the mavis and blackbird also used those runs, and it was sickening and painful to find one of those song birds trapped by both legs, the lovely feathers blood-stained and drab in death.

But rats' blood did not upset us, nor did the frequent tatters of skin around the trap, where the captive had been attacked and eaten by his free companions. At times, too, we would find the trap with only a paw and the shank of a leg where the rat had gnawed through his own leg, and gone off to die slowly somewhere else.

Rats generally are very wary and cunning, and I have no doubt that those we caught were in the heat of the chase or the fight, as frequently we could hear them fighting and squealing as they chased each other madly, banging against the corrugated walls of the washhouse. They were mostly male, and we rarely caught a female. There seemed to be about twenty males to one female, and that would seem to be nature's way of keeping their numbers in bounds, as they breed very rapidly.

The gamekeepers would sometimes have a purge of the rats. They went round all the burrows, throwing into them neat little sandwiches of bread, with fat and phosphorus. It was said that the phosphorus made them very thirsty, and then when they drank, the water activated the poison and killed them. We were always warned when the gamekeepers were on a poison round, in order to keep the hens locked up until all the sandwiches had been eaten by those for whom they were intended. Inevitably, there were accidents. One of the hens would pick up a piece of the bread, carried out of a burrow and left exposed.

When that happened, Heaven help the first gamekeeper my mother ran into. The enraged woman tore into him tooth and nail. The hen would be locked into the washhouse and prevented from drinking. It was pitiful to see the poor creature running its beak along the ground and going through the motions of drinking. It would be dosed with lumps of oatmeal and butter stuffed down its throat, for several days. If the bird had been been found soon enough, and the treatment started straight away, it usually recovered, but it was a long time before it got back to its business of egg laying.

I was always fascinated by rats, and have spent a lot of time and thought in trying to outwit them.

There was one hoary old scrounger who was in the habit of picking up scraps in front of the bothy window, and I decided to test his intelligence with a trap. I left it lying in the open, unbaited and sprung. I watched as he approached, quite unafraid, and gave it a good examination. I then baited and set it, and went back to watch again. His tactics were remarkable, and showed a degree of intelligence that no doubt had enabled him to reach a hoary old age. His approach this time was very wary and suspicious. He circled the trap a few times, sniffing at the morsel of bait. Then he stepped back and poised for a leap. He jumped high over the trap, and as he did so flicked it with his tail. At the third or fourth leap, he was successful: the trap sprang shut and he seemed to know that all was now safe. He calmly went up and ate the bait.

But not all rats were as brainy as that old chap. I recall one that was either excessively stupid or quite insensitive to pain. He had been eating the potatoes, so I set a cage trap for him, one end of which was a spring loaded door. The next morning I was very surprised to find the trap sprung and all the bait eaten, but no trapped rat. Somehow he had been inside, eaten the bait and got out again. This went on for several nights even after I had put a heavier spring on the door. Eventually, I gave up, and conceded victory to the animal.

Some time later I trapped a creature which I had some difficulty in recognising as a rat, so big was he and so disfigured. The whole face had been rubbed off up to the roots of his ears.   The eyes were gone and the upper lip, and the skull and teeth were exposed.   This was my old enemy, and all the damage had been done night after night as he forced his way under the heavily sprung cage door to escape after eating the bait.   He had virtually removed the whole of his face in the process.

I had many other experiences with rats, which, as I have said, always had a strange fascination for me.   In a very minor way they represented for me what the bigger animals represented for the Gentry.   Our sport came much cheaper, though.

THE GENTRY

Thinking back to the time when Sir George and Lady Bullough (she was never referred to as Lady Monica) reigned on the Island of Rhum, it now amazes me to realise what little contact we had with them. By 'we' I mean the common herd. The Gentry had their personal servants and attendants, of course, but they lived a life as exclusive as that of their employers, and seldom left the policies to mingle with the natives. When they were not on duty, the maids and other servants would stroll about the gardens, where we would sometimes catch a glimpse of them making vain attempts to defend themselves against the ever-present and savage midges, who were delighted to make the most of this luscious new blood, drawing it through the delicate and unweathered skin of the dainty maidens.

The servants would sometimes linger near the massive white gates dividing them from us, and gaze through at the outside world, and, I have no doubt, wondered what sort of strange creatures inhabited it.

Those gates were the barriers that kept us out, rather than keeping them in. We looked on the Castle servants as beings from another world, but would gladly have dallied with them, when we had reached dallying age.

It was all a bit like some great beehive within that barrier, with the Queen Bee and her attendants sacrosanct within, with the attendants humming and buzzing about, serving Her Majesty, while we workers ensured that the inner sanctum was secure and well provided for.

Sir George, accompanied by his head gamekeeper, would occasionally be seen making off for the hill, followed by the ghillie leading the pony, which we all hoped would come back with a stag on its back. The ghillie was usually my father, who, if there were no more pressing duties, followed the laird on his expeditions.

Apart from those sporting (and predominantly male) excursions, the occupants of the beehive were seldom seen. If any of them did venture out, we, the workers, were expected, even obliged, to scurry into whatever refuge we could find until the entourage had passed. If we were not smart enough and an unexpected encounter did happen, Lady Bullough was always very friendly and gracious, and would stop and have a short chat.

She was invariably accompanied by her daughter, Hermione, who, strangely enough, during her mother's conversation, repeated her every word and gesture. My mother said that this was training for her future social life. To us, it merely served to widen the gap between 'Us' and 'Them'. Certainly it was quite disconcerting to hear her Ladyship speak, and then listen to the echo!

I daresay Hermione did find this early training useful, if indeed that was what it was, because later she married and became Lady Durham.

Sir George was always quite friendly, and would pass the time of day, but he had the rather austere air which he thought appropriate to the Highland laird, a role he tried hard to play to the full. He would frequently visit the steading to inspect the ponies which were kept in loose boxes for breeding.

The only occasion I can remember Lady Bullough and her daughter visiting that area was when they came down to make the acquaintance of a white nanny goat which had been imported with the express purpose of providing milk to build up Hermione, who was tall, willowy and delicate-looking. Somebody had the bright idea that goat's milk was the very stuff to do the job.

Perhaps she did not drink enough of it, because when the milk supply dried up, Hermione still looked the same. She might have grown a bit, but that was all. The poor white goat, having done its bit as a body-builder, surely deserved a better fate than what befell it. There was no leisurely retirement for it, no growing old graciously. Without a word of thanks or appreciation, she was turned loose in Harris Glen, the most inhospitable and desolate area of the whole island, where there was already a flock of wild goats. The poor beast had never seen a bog or a crag, and I am quite sure would not have recognised any of those black and hairy beasts as relatives of hers, far less as possible mates. Anyway, she did not last long: indeed, she did not survive the first cold blast of winter.

Perhaps it had been hoped that the white goat would improve the breed of the wild goats, just as it was hoped that the imported white stallion would improve the breed of our native ponies. Neither thing happened. Their blood was just too thin for the harshness of life on Rhum outside the sheltered grounds of the Castle.

I did have rather closer contact with Hermione one day, and, true to all romances, fell in love with her. I don't think she reciprocated, but I shall never really know, because we never had another chance of meeting until many years later, when it was far too late. She and her companion were on the beach that day, and I joined them, and very pleasant it was too. My mother witnessed this fraternising, and I got a severe dressing-down for it, and a lecture on my un-serflike behaviour, as well as a severe warning about never repeating it. Such warnings from my mother were rare enough to make us all regard them with a great deal of awe, and they were never disregarded. Just the same, had the opportunity ever presented itself, which it didn't, I just might have disregarded that one, for I was in love. But the lassie was always chaperoned, and I had to be satisfied with worshipping her from a distance.

The only real fraternising between 'them' and 'us' were on such occasions as school prize day and the yearly sports. The White Gates were opened then, and the policies open to everyone, Gentry and commoner alike. They were days to be treasured and talked about for a long time, but when the day was over, we all reverted to our proper stations. Certainly we did not resent this, at the time, and simply and unquestioningly accepted them as Superior Beings.

I never figured anywhere in the school prize giving, and I never did very well, either, in the sports. But there was a reason for that. After all, I was fleet of foot, and could outpace most lads. The reason was that some of us had discovered that there was a way into the refreshment tent under the walls, and the refreshment tent was deserted during each of the events, although it filled up quickly enough during the intervals. We were in there during the races and other events, mopping up everything we could find left on the bar and the tables, and certainly were in no condition to give of our best in any juvenile races.

There was one time the factor got himself stuck on top of some barrier during an obstacle race. He was not, naturally, a popular figure, and everyone was out there to watch his struggles, and perhaps hoping that he would slip. He didn't slip, and eventually got down safely, with only his dignity and pride hurt, but we had made the most of his struggles, and had a most thorough clean up in the refreshment tent. There were some very puzzled faces, and not a few recriminations, when the crowd surged back in there, to find that all their drinks and eats had disappeared.

MIDGES

Although I might be prejudiced in this, I really believe that perhaps the most remarkable character on Rhum in those days was my own father. I cannot really vouch for all the stories he told us of his exploits as a young man, and perhaps he embellished them a little, but certainly he did not embellish the tale of how he caught the stag. It needed no embellishment, and anyway, I was there for at least part of the time.

Usually, while we children were being prepared for bed, my father would go out, as he said, to look at the stars. In fact, he generally went down to the bothy, to have a crack with the bachelors who lived there, but on one particular night he went out with the determination to go poaching.

My father was no weakling, either in mind or body, in fact he was a very strong man, and for the task he had in mind he would need all his strength. On leaving the house, he went into the shed and picked up a heavy rasp file. He could never explain why he did that, and always maintained that he was under Divine Guidance!

He then made his way to the gate through the dry stone dyke, and into the area around the henhouse, where the hens were fed. There were always bits and pieces lying about there, bits too big for the hens to swallow. (Hens, unlike seagulls, are poor swallowers. I have seen a seagull pick up a dead rat by the nose and swallow it whole, and fly off with the rat's tail sticking out of its beak.) Whatever titbits were left by the hens were eagerly sought by the deer, who came snuffling around after dark. Usually they were up on the hills by day, but came down after dark for any easy pickings.

When my father went through the wobbly wee gate, there was a scuffling on the hens' feeding ground. The deer were there, and they fled, with my father after them. If there had been anyone to see it, I suppose it would have been amusing, with this big man pounding along over the rough ground, leaping boulders and tussocks, splashing through bogs, while the deer leapt easily over all obstacles, and got much further in front.

There was a dilapidated wire fence round the area, and the deer made for it, to escape the terror that was after them. All but one cleared the fence easily enough, but a straggler caught its leg in the top wire. Seeing this, my father made an extra effort and as the beast freed itself, he managed to grab a hind leg. It might all have been, as he maintained, Divine Guidance, and he was going to need all of that there was going. He never remembered clearing the fence himself, but did, and then there was the deer on its home ground, hell-bent for its freedom, and my father, hanging on as it tore over the rough ground on three legs. Eventually, the beast slowed down, and father was able to get alongside and hit it over the back of the head with his heavy rasp.

Once was enough, and the beast fell. So did my father, for a few minutes, while he got his breathing under control, and considered what to do next. It was clear enough — he had to get the beast home. So he hoisted it on his back and went home.

We heard father returning from his nightly inspection of the stars, but it was a very dishevelled and mud-spattered figure that appeared at the living room door and signalled my mother to come out. There was no argument. She dropped whatever it was she was doing and went.

In a few minutes she was back, obviously excited, and scuttled about, getting the children to bed quickly, not like the usual bedtime fun and games and nonsense. As the oldest boy, I got the wink to stay behind. My own poaching habits were well enough established, even if a bit immature, and I was let into most such ploys.

As soon as we got outside into the darkness I could smell deer, and realised that there was something big happening. Indeed, there was: a whole deer to ourselves.

Between us, we dragged the carcase into the kitchen, hoisted it on to two chairs and did the necessary skinning and butchering. The debris, and there wasn't much of that, was carried out and buried in the garden. We had no 'lanterns dimly burning' for this. It had to be carried out in total darkness, and we went out again at first light to make sure there were no incriminating bits left lying around. That was most important, because Donald MacGillivray lived next door, and he was a gamekeeper, the dedicated enemy of poachers. Donald was a decent chap, as gamekeepers go, and I feel sure he would not have shopped us, but signs of nocturnal activity would have aroused his suspicions, and there was no need to get him involved if it could be avoided. Knowing Donald, I am sure that if he had learned of our offence (even crime), he would have been burdened with guilt for the rest of his life.

Donald, incidentally, after he left the island, carried out a good deal of efficient poaching on his own. It really was a case of the gamekeeper turned poacher. He showed me how to doctor small calibre ammunition to make it more effective against deer, and told me where to hit the animal to make sure of a kill. That was precision poaching, and required a lot of skill and daring, but it paled into insignificance when compared with my father's feat of running down and capturing a deer on its own ground, on a dark night, and killing it with a rasp!

When we discussed it all the next day, when things had returned to something like normal, there seemed to be some justification for father's claim to have been under Divine Guidance. Why did he go into the shed and pick up a rasp? How did he know there was a whole herd on the other side of the dyke? What forlorn hope induced him to follow the animals? Finally, why was one of them entangled in the fence, a fence they must have cleared half a hundred times? You can reason it out as you will: we were satisfied with the venison without enquiring too deeply into the way it was placed on our plates. It lasted a long time.

Killing a deer, of course, was a great crime on the island. Indeed, I cannot think of any greater. The stag was King, and Royal Game. He was the core around which all other activities revolved. Although the factor and his minions had vast powers, these, fortunately, fell short of decapitation, otherwise that would certainly have been done to anyone known to have killed a stag. Such illegal killing was tantamount to regicide.

The factor had such powers that even for a minor offence, or even because of a dislike of the person concerned, there could be instant dismissal and expulsion from the island. That was a serious business, because the whole family was deported, lock, stock and barrel, and if they did not have relatives on the mainland to take them in, they were in serious trouble.

My father, though, stayed there for many more years without any regrets over his action. Perhaps he accepted only fifty per cent of the blame, with the rest credited to the Divine Guidance.

Apart from the factors, the chief bane of life on Rhum was certainly the midges, which seemed to be a particularly virulent and persistent strain. Experts say that midges don't like sunshine and don't go out to sea, and the experts are wrong on both counts. Many is the time I have been plagued with them when well out to sea, and I can certainly attest to the positive liking the Rhum midge has for sunshine.

There was one day I was passing a field where three men were scything hay. It was a very hot day, with brilliant sunshine, and I knew the men must be very uncomfortable, for they were wearing fine muslin veils as protection against the midges. The clouds of midges were so dense that it was difficult to breathe without such protection. But it was almost as bad wearing them, because they soon became almost sealed up with condensation and sweat.

What puzzled me on that particular day, though, was that each man seemed to be carrying a sheet of glass on his back. When I moved closer to satisfy my curiosity about this, I was amazed to find that what I had mistaken for sheets of glass was in fact the sun shining on the wings of a solid mass of midges.

There are many songs extolling the glories of the 'Good Old Summer Time', but there can be few more ghastly experiences than hand weeding on a summer's morning at about six o'clock. Of course, the midges were there before us. Perhaps they had been lying in wait from the previous evening, but they were there right enough, hungry and ready for action as we donned our muslin veils. The dew would wet our hands, the dust from the dry soil would stick to them and rise into the air, and soon our veils were almost air-tight. When we raised them briefly, to get a breath of air, we found that air impregnated with midges. Replacing the veil trapped a number of the little tormentors, and from then on, it was either suffocate or breath midges and scratch, until we were splattered with mud and blood. We lads wore knickerbockers, not yet having graduated to the height of adult long trousers, and the gap between the bottom of our knickerbockers and the top of our stockings was exposed, and a favourite feeding ground. It was soon a strip of lacerated flesh and mud. We did not complain, for their was no use in complaining, and anyway we had grown up with those conditions, and knew no other.

That wasn't so with one of our gardeners, a companion in distress. John MacLean had been a butler until he fell to the Demon Drink, as many butlers do. As a butler, he had known an easier and more comfortable way of life than his present existence as garden labourer, and could not easily accept the conditions as we did, and his constant stream of invective, directed at his miniscule tormentors, was colourful and licentious.

He was always the perfect gentleman when off duty, and maintained the style of his previous life and dressed immaculately. John was a first class performer on the Jews' (Properly Jaw's) harp, or tump, and often entertained us in the bothy with reels and strathspeys on that simple instrument which is so difficult to play. But the tirade which poured out in Gaelic and the description of all midges and their ancestors was not couched in his usual gentlemanly terms: then, he was talking like a garden labourer.   Poor John, he was an irascible but entertaining character.

There was one day when his annual leave had come round, and John, well primed and dressed in the style of one of his erst-while employers, was making his way to the pier to board the boat to take him to Tobermory.   As he strolled along, swinging his home-made walking stick (another craft at which he excelled), he would pause occasionally and give voice to a verse of two of a Gaelic song, while he gazed around on this beautiful summer morning, the first day of his holiday.   He was cutting it pretty neat, and one of the ferry men was sent along to try to give him some sense of urgency.   But John was not moved by the urgings to 'Come on, John, or you'll miss the boat!'

John stepped back, removed his hat with a flourish, and in the best butler manner made a gracious bow and requested, in the best boudoir accent: 'Will you please kiss my arse.'   He was in no mood for advice, and he missed the boat and a whole week of his holidays.

Incidentally, if you think I exaggerate the ferocity of the Rhum midges, there was one case in which a man died from their bites.   It was long before my time, and indeed happened in the old days, but the story was still repeated, and there was some evidence that it was true.

There is an old road to Kilmory from Kinloch, running along the north side of the glen, and halfway along, at a place called *Araidh Thalmhuinn* (Place of the Yarrow) there stands a small uninscribed headstone, which we knew as 'The Baby's Grave.'   This was one of our favorite walks, and often enough I heard my father tell the story as we stood there.

It was all long ago, in the time of the chiefs, and when the baby daughter of the chief died, he instructed two of his trusted men to carry the coffin to Kilmory for burial.   With only half their journey completed, a severe thunderstorm came on, and the two men decided to go no further, but to bury the baby where they were, and say nothing about it.

But the two men fell out about something, and the facts were revealed. The chief was exceedingly angry, especially at the man, his trusted servant, who had been in charge of the burial. The man was stripped and pegged out on the grass, at the place where the school now stands. The chief's wife, still mourning the death of her baby daughter, believed that such revenge was too harsh, and pleaded with her husband for mercy. He relented, and the man was released, but too late, for he had been so sorely bitten by the midges of Rhum that he died in agony anyway.

One of the most noteworthy characters on the island was Alexander McMillan, known as 'Old Sandy'. He was an immensely strong man, and on account of this, and other things, had quite a reputation in his native island of Skye, so much so that in his youth he had been nicknamed *Alister an Seareich* —Alister the Colt.

He was one of the leaders in the defence of the rights of the crofters of Skye, and in the Battle of the Braes. As we were told the story, an attempt had been made by the landlord (who incidentally, was not a foreign incomer, but Lord MacDonald himself) to evict the crofters from an area which had been occupied by them for generations. When local authority failed to drive the crofters out, a contingent of the Glasgow Police was called in to help.

It was no secret that they were coming, and Sandy prepared for the invasion. He had all the human waste in the village collected, and stored up a good supply of this ammunition, which was kept by the upstairs window of Sandy's croft. When the police and the local authorities arrived, Sandy and his wife had a good view of them as they gathered round his barred door. They were given plenty of time to congregate before Sandy whispered to his wife (in Gaelic, of course): 'Bring the pots, Lexie. Bring the pots and buckets. They're here!'

In his relating of this event, Sandy would at this point burst into chortles of glee, as he told how he let the forces of law and order have the contents of the buckets and pots. There was a rapid and messy and smelly withdrawal, and the first round went to Sandy. He did go to prison for a short spell as a result of the Battle of the Braes, but just the same it was one of the final events that led eventually to the Crofters Act, and security for their holdings.

Of course, all this happened before he came to Rhum, but he was still a very powerful man, and at the Highland Games he could be seen strutting about the lawns, the tug-of-war rope wound round his massive shoulders, shouting after each victory: 'That's the fresh herring boys done! Bring on the next lot!.'

Even with his long white beard, he was a power to be reckoned with, and would tackle anything. It was always Sandy who would be lowered over the cliff to any sheep that had got down there, and that was a frequent occurence.

Once, two sheep were marooned on a ledge above a sheer drop of several hundred feet to the sea. There was no call for volunteers. There was no need, for Sandy was there. He was lowered over the cliff and reached the narrow ledge on which the animals were trapped. He gripped the first one and grappled it up under his oxter, then shouted to the men at the top to haul him up. With Sandy's feet actually off the ledge, the remaining animal made a dash for what it thought would be freedom, but which could only have ended with a smashed body on the rocks far below. As it passed beneath his feet, Sandy made a grab and sank his gnarled fingers into the wool of its back. In that way, he and both sheep were hauled up to safety. And those were not the little sheep we know today, but big old wedders which had gone virtually wild and had not been handled since they were lambs, some years earlier.

Sandy was still married to Lexie, but she was in Skye, attending to the croft, and on Rhum he lived in the bothy provided for single men. I never met Lexie, but I believe she was a fit wife for the grand man, and as hard working as he was. There is a story of the Skyeman who, glum-faced, was met by a friend, who enquired the reason for the gloom. 'Ach, well,' he was told, 'It's the end of the year, the ploughing's not done, and if I don't get married before spring I'll need to buy a horse.' Nothing like that applied to Sandy.

He did not associate much with younger occupants of the bothy, but spent much time in his own room, reading his Bible, and was respected, even feared, by all.

Sandy ran a sort of miniature shop from his bedroom, in which he sold some of the bare essentials such as tea, sugar and salt herring, a large barrel of those being kept behind the bothy. They were not always very fresh, that I do remember, and the bothy lads had insisted that the barrel be moved outside.

Some lads, of which I was one, raided his store one day when we found the door unlocked and helped ourselves to handfuls of sugar from the large bag standing in the corner. As it happened, we had previously gorged ourselves on raw turnips pulled from the nearby field, and peeled with a sharp stone, in the stone-age manner. Any lad who had a knife would have been in the capitalist class, if not downright Gentry. I had one eventually, but that was years later. I vividly remember that night, as, felled to the knees, I gazed at what came out of my overloaded stomach. It was not a pretty sight, and put me off both raw sugar and turnips for a long time. Even the digestion of young lads seems to have some limits.

Old Sandy was a bit gruff and not easily approachable, but he had a kindly streak and would at times bring us out a bag of sweets from what we thought of as his Aladdin's Cave. This was a real treat for us, as there were no sweets to be bought on the island.

But Old Sandy's speciality was fried seagull eggs, which were free and plentiful during the breeding season. After his annual foray to the nesting grounds, about five miles away, he would arrive home with a load of questionable booty, and sometimes allow us to take part in the resulting feast. Sandy usually went on his own, but sometimes went with us on our own expeditions for seagull eggs. But we were careful in our collecting and were advised to take eggs from nests which contained less than three eggs, since the gull lays three eggs to a clutch, and any less than that meant that they were fairly fresh. Old Sandy was not selective, and took everything that fell to his hand.

Back at the bothy, he would produce his big frying pan, black with

137

the grease of a thousand meals cooked over the open fire. He would crack the eggs on the edge of the pan and slosh the contents into the smoking fat, which was probably venison, highly ripe and well matured. Most of the eggs would be in perfect condition. Many would not and there would be quite a few bits of seagull in the first flush .of youth, you might say. Quite undismayed, Sandy would guddle about with his fork, and anything showing signs of advanced incubation, like a beak, would be removed with the fork and flicked into the ashpan. It was all still good eating, and Sandy made grand, de-embryo-ed omelettes with those seagull eggs.

Sandy liked all his food in its natural state, and I have seen him wrench out a handful of growing oats, put the heads in his mouth and, pulling at the straw, rip the grain off with his teeth. He would then eat the lot, chaff, husks and grain, with the juice trickling down his beard. I once saw him attempting to evict a stag from a fenced plantation of young trees. At times the infuriated animal would turn and charge, and Sandy would be off like a moose, old man as he was, with the antlers inches away from his backside. He plunged into any convenient clump of scrub until the chase had cooled down. He got the stag out, though. In all his encounters, with man or beast, Old Sandy rarely came second.

I am afraid that the hooligan element, of which I was a prominent member, did not treat Old Sandy with the respect he very properly deserved, and that is something I have long regretted. I could have learned much from him, and perhaps some of his character would have rubbed off on me. In fact, we were often cheeky in our response to his attempts to be sociable and conversational. He usually accepted our impudence in silence, and just walked away. He stunned us one day, though.

It was the last day of school, and we had been released for the summer holidays, following the annual grilling by the visiting inspector. This was always a strain on pupils and teachers alike, and we were vaunty at having escaped unscathed from the grilling. We came on Old Sandy digging a hole at the side of the road. He stopped work, and, leaning on his shovel, in a quiet and friendly manner, congratulated us on being so well dressed, and asked us about our performanace before the inspector. We gave cheeky and insulting replies to him, and he was driven beyond the limit. He laid down his shovel and leaned forward, hands gripping the edge of the hole in which he was standing. With great venom he spat out: 'And did he not put his finger up your arses to find your brains there?' We were indeed stunned and silenced as he disappeared into the hole, and we heard his muffled laughter.

In his youth, Sandy had been one of the strongest men on Skye. At the annual gathering there, the lads of the village always tested their strength by lifting a large boulder. That lifting contest was in fact the last remnant of an old clan ceremony, in which all the fighting men had to prove their fitness by lifting a boulder, which was kept for the purpose. Anyway, each year when he went home for the harvest and the gathering, Sandy would have his own set-to with the boulder,just to prove himself. In the year before he retired from Rhum, he came back from his holiday very depressed. He had tried repeatedly, but had been unable to lift the stone. He should not really have been dismayed, as he was then well over seventy, how much over, we did not know and it would have been hard to guess, for he was always 'Old Sandy' tough and aggressive.

There were some language problems on the island. Of course, at home we were Gaelic speakers until we went to school, when we learned English, and soon were able to reply to our Gaelic-speaking parents in that new language. But the English we learned was not always that of some who worked on the island. Some of them spoke the broad Lowland Scots or some dialect of English. I remember one incomer who asked one of the boys 'Is yer fether a jiner?' Had he asked 'Is your father a joiner?' we would probably have understood, for that was the English we were learning, but this was surely a joke, and we laughed about it, thinking he was being funny. The poor man walked off in disgust. We adopted those new words, and used them in our various conflicts. They almost sounded like a war-cry as they resounded from both sides: 'Is yer fether a jiner, fether a jiner, fether a jiner!' It was something new in our vocabulary, and we revelled in it.

THE END OF IT ALL

During his time, Sir George made many visits to Rhum, mostly in the autumn, accompanied by a party of his sporting friends. They came in the autumn, because that was the time for stalking the deer. Some of his friends were not very proficient at shooting, even if keen to experience the 'adventurous' life on an island in the wilds of Scotland. Those neophytes would be put through a preliminary training session before being taken on the hill to pit their skill with a rifle against a defenceless stag.

Some of those sportsmen would prove to be a sore trial to the stalker and gamekeeper, who were frequently left to track a badly wounded beast for miles over the hills, for it was a matter of honour that all shot beasts had to be killed. Sometimes they had to give up the chase when darkness fell, and resume it the next day.

In an effort to reduce such events, all unknown quantities with a rifle were taken out to the moor behind the White House, where an iron model of a stag had been set up. Under the guidance and direction of a gamekeeper, the tenderfeet were instructed to blaze away at that until they were considered ready to be turned loose with a reasonable chance of making a kill.

The elation of the stalker was sometimes damped, as he stood admiring his trophy. If it was his first kill, he was 'blooded', much to his surprise, by having a handful of the deer's blood dashed in his face. It certainly made a bit of a mess, and the lady 'firsts' were not exempt. They were very concerned about the state of their new sporting gear, and less worried about the blood dripping from their chin. Had they but known it, they had no reason for alarm, for deer blood, if allowed to dry, will rub off like powder. Having recovered from this, they were all delighted and full of bravado, striding home behind the loaded ponies.

On a really good day, three stags would be taken home, and two stags on one pony was a really heavy load over the rough and marshy ground. But those ponies never seemed to put a foot wrong.

If there were three stags, instead of the more usual one, or even none, it meant a very long day for the ghillies and gamekeepers, who had already spent hours on the hill. The arrival of the ponies carrying the carcases was a welcome sight to us, who hung around, savouring the smell of hot leather, sweating horses and the smell of the deer themselves, which of course meant venison, our main food in the stalking season.

After a quick bite to eat, the ghillies and gamekeepers started the work, which often carried them late into the night. The beasts had been 'gralloched' (disembowelled and bled) on the hill, but all the skinning and butchering had to be done. We youngsters helped wherever we could, but I think we were probably more of a hindrance than a help really, as the skilled men hustled about, weighing and dressing the carcases by the flickering light of the lanterns, and surrounded by clouds of our malicious midges.

What really kept us hanging about was the anticipation of fried liver and onions. One of the lucky loiterers, perhaps because of his patience and perseverance, would be given a stag's liver, which, fried with onions, is still, to me, one of the most luscious foods on earth.

When the carcases had been dressed and hung up, and the whole place hosed down, we youngsters were sent off, the one carrying the liver running faster than the rest, in a hurry to show his treasure at home. The ghillies and gamekeepers would make their way to the gunroom at the castle, to enjoy a drink and a crack. There was plenty of real beer on tap there, and it was free, and they could regale each other with tales of other days, of other stalks, of points and weights. My father was amongst them, and when they had left the castle, there would be a few Gaelic songs to give the finishing touch to a most satisfactory day. My father more than once arrived home quite convivial after those sessions in the gunroom, to get a tirade from his wife (Wee Free, and disapproving), and his reward of a good dish of liver and onions.

But it was not all blood, booze, midges and fried liver after a day on the hill. Lady Bullough was not particularly enthusiastic about Rhum and the sporting life it provided. She was French and very much a socialite, and enjoyed a bit of chit-chat and gossip. Her first call on arriving at the island was invariably at our house. My mother had been in the service of the Bulloughs for many years, and the two of them could gabble away all afternoon enquiring about each other's friends.

Although Lady Bullough did not take to the hill, as some of her female contemporaries did, she did not lack entertainment. While the tougher of them crawled the hill, chasing a stag, those at home chased a golf ball around the course laid out in the policies surrounding the castle. Later, after the returned hunting heroes and heroines had removed the mud and the blood, they would join the rest of the party for pre-dinner drinks, and no doubt greatly exaggerated tales of the chase.

Meanwhile, the head gardener and myself, after I had left school and become a gardening apprentice, would be decorating the dining table with some sort of exotic and flowery lay-out. Percy Hills was a master at this, and some of his creations were really beautiful. We were not popular with the maids and the housekeeper, though, nor did they appreciate our efforts. We left stains on the tablecloths. There were no modern materials for setting up our displays, so we fell back on what we certainly had in abundance, and that was peat. We used slabs of that convenient stuff, but it did make a mess. We changed all the designs each day, so perhaps the complaints were justified. But they were lovely displays, and we thought so, anyway, when we received effusive thanks from Her Ladyship.

After the port and cigars had gone their rounds and the day's activities embellished upon, the gentlemen would join the ladies, and all would make their way to the ballroom, to dance through the night, under the heavenly blue ceiling, with its starry decorations shining through, to the music of that amazing contraption, the electric organ.

Well, it is all gone now. There is no more dancing in the ballroom: the electric organ is silent and that whole remarkable society that revolved round Sir George and his Lady has gone into the mists.

The end began, as did so many other ends, in nineteen-fourteen. There was no more rattling of pots and pans, no more anguished shrieks from the chef, no more of those tantalising smells. Gone was the delicious roast beef dripping we collected every week and spread thick on home made oatcakes. There was no butter like that!

Everything was replaced by preparations for war. The Albions and the carriages were packed away for the last time in their dust sheets. All the young men, including the fourteen gardeners who maintained those glorious policies, were mustered. The riding ponies were assembled with all the harness — some of it quite unused.

Those gardeners were made into cavalrymen, although most of them had hardly touched, let alone ridden, a horse. They were hoisted up and in turns walked and trotted and cantered round the castle until they were considered capable of hanging on. They then disappeared like a cloud of midges in a breeze of wind to display in the mud of Flanders what they had learned in a quick canter around the castle on the island of Rhum. Mostly they are still in Flanders.

There were only the boys left, of which I was one, to maintain the gardens and the greenhouses, and gradually the grapes, the peaches and the orchids vanished, gradually sliding into the wilderness of weeds and broken glass that marks their position today.

I don't intend to get involved in discussion about the rights and wrongs of big estates. Really, that is quite pointless, since there are so few of them left. But this I know: the estate of Rhum employed about a hundred people, and they were better off there than they would have been almost anywhere else. Of course it was a patriarchal and even tyrannical society in which we grew up, but I would rather have grown up there, with all the freedom and beauty of the island, than in some Gorbals slum.

Sir George died suddenly, on a golf course in France, and was taken back to Rhum, which he loved so dearly, to be buried at Harris. His wife, Lady Monica, died a lonely woman, and was also taken back to lie beside her husband. I stood on the hillside at Corpach as the train went by carrying the mortal remains of a most gracious lady to her last resting place, beside her husband, the late Laird of Rhum, on the stormy shore at Harris.

I raised my hat and held it there until the sound of the train died away, and ended an era to which we can never return.

POSTSCRIPT

I left Rhum in 1920 at the age of seventeen. It was not a voluntary move. The factor Brebner sacked me after I protested to Sir George about being fined £1 by the factor for taking a boat without his permission. My wage at the time was ten shillings a week, and when I protested, I learned later, my protest did not even reach Sir George, but was passed back by the secretary to be dealt with by the factor himself. So it was a month's notice for me, and the £1 deducted from the wages due. Perhaps if that had not happened, I would have stayed on the island for as long as my father did.

So, I had a month in which to find new employment and somewhere to live, for I had to leave the island. Reading *The Oban Times*, my mother picked on an advertisment which seemed to suit me. It was over the pseudonymn 'Delve', and was for a gardener at Inverlochy Castle, near Fort William. Well, I knew how to 'delve' alright. More than once I had been set to delve a half acre of kitchen garden. That was a devil of a task for a boy on his own, and to shorten the slavery I devised a system whereby I went back a few yards and took out some spadefuls of soil and threw it over a large area of undug ground, making it look as though it had been turned over. Whoever planted that ground must have had a difficult job.

I got the job at Inverlochy, and before leaving the island on which I had spent all my life I went around to all my favorite places. With a friend I walked up the Harris road and there, at the junction with the Kilmory road we sat down in the sunshine and I carved my name deep into the red rock at the roadside, *Archie Cameron*, and it can still be seen there today, more than seventy years later.

It was a sad day for my mother, I know, as she watched the first of her brood leave the nest. She stood at the front door waving a bedsheet until the steamer rounded the point on its way to Mallaig and my destiny. That became a regular ritual when we were leaving home.

The train journey from Mallaig to Fort William was strange. It was the first time I had been in a train, and that was a great excitement. The scenery was new and exciting, and there seemed to be crowds of unknown people getting in and leaving the train at each of the tiny stations. Would the train stop at Fort William? Would I recognise it? Well, it did and I did, and then had a walk of three miles to the castle. The whole day had been one of trauma, but I was really too excited about it all to feel much sadness then. That came later.

A cousin of my father's was married to the home farm manager, and that was a godsend. At least I had a friendly fireside sometimes, and somewhere to have my washing done. The washing was the hardest part, for me, of living in the bothy. I could cope with the cooking, but I had never had to wash a single garment in my life — mother had taken care of that. There was another distant cousin around, too, and he was a postman. That meant he had a bicycle, and he taught me to ride. It wasn't too easy, and often enough I fell off where there was no convenient tree to support me as I remounted. That meant I had to walk home, pushing the bike.

Eventually, though, I became proficient enough, and then bought a bike of my own. What joy! I toured the Lochaber countryside for miles in every direction. Even snow did not stop me.

My letters home were full of the new things I was seeing, and some of those new things were quite astonishing to me. My first letter described in detail my first meeting with a frog, and I even attempted a drawing of it. I had never seen a frog before, but it could not have amazed my parents as much as it did me: they had seen it all before.

But it was chocolate which thrilled me more than anything else. In all my sixteen years I had never seen, let alone eaten, a bar of chocolate, and here there was a whole world filled with them. Every

147

penny of my very meagre pocket money went on them, and I gorged. I would walk the three miles along the railway track to Fort William night after night, just to fill my pocket with penny bars from those magic machines on the railway station.

As a lad raw from the islands, I committed some bloomers in my first weeks on the mainland. One of them, strangely enough, concerned girls. For some reason, perhaps just because I was so very innocent, I seemed to attract the attention of several girls around the castle and the farms. Looking back at it later, I was amazed that they buzzed around so much, and I was regretful that so many chances had been lost. More surprisingly, when I became a bit more mature about girls, and actually started a bit of chasing myself, I found that my attraction for them had vanished. Perhaps it was the youthful innocent they sought, not the sophisticated man of the world I imagined I had become.

Again, there was the matter of the barber. I had never been to a barber's shop in my life, of course, and I have already told how my father did all that was necessary in that department. The time came, though, when I had to have a haircut, and did just as we used to do at home. Jacket, collar, and tie all came off, just as they did at home, but I was unable to straddle the chair and had to be content with sitting in it. The barber was rather surprised by all this, of course, and so were the waiting customers. I got my haircut alright, but could hear the laughter from well down the street as I left the shop with what dignity I could. I had learned something new about those peculiar people who did not live on islands, and of how they were inconsiderate of their best clothes and did not mind getting short hairs on their jackets and shirts.

I did not stay long at Inverlochy. The castle was closed down, the policies allowed to run down, and I was on the road. Not for long, though, and I found myself at Castle Toward, down by Dunoon. This place was one of those owned by the Coates family of Paisley, makers of thread and cloth, and so wealthy that they seemed to be unaffected by the sort of financial paralysis aflicting Lord Abinger of Inverlochy.

Many changes were being made at Castle Toward, and the place swarmed with workmen and gardeners. However, I had not been long there before I was struck down with appendicitis and a ruptured appendix.

Actually, the appendicitis had struck me before, at Inverlochy, and it was bad enough to make me visit the doctor, something I had never done before. He thought I had eaten a piece of hard potato, and advised me to eat my tatties mashed from then on. I thought as little of his advice as of him: he had not spent the previous night in the Inverlochy bothy sweating with pain and chewing on a handkerchief to stop the groans. So I kept on eating my tatties boiled and not mashed, and hoped that never again would I suffer that sort of pain.

I did, though, at Castle Toward, and it was even worse. I was really hoping that death would come and end it. In the morning, the woman from the lodge came along, and dosed me with 'Health Salts', which was without doubt the worst possible thing that could have happened. The doctor came out from Inellan, and then sent me off to Dunooon hospital in a rickety old taxi. By this time, the appendix had burst, and it was far from a pleasant journey. A surgeon came over from Glasgow the next day and attempted to clear up the mess.

When I came round, my bed was enclosed by red screens, which even I, who had never even seen a hospital before, knew was not a good thing. I had been packed with about fifty yards of gauze, and it was changed every day, being pushed deep into my gut with what looked for all the world like a spirtle. There were no antibiotics then, of course, and nature and the patient were left to sort it all out between themselves. Whatever was being sorted out in my gut certainly caused some quite obnoxious smells, and the nurse would pour a bottle of *eau de Cologne* over my bed during visiting hours. After ten weeks of this, my father arrived to take me home, and I went back to Rhum, the best of all possible places to convalesce. While I was there, some sort of financial blizzard must have hit the world of thread and cloth, for the Coates family shut down Toward, and I was again looking out for a job.

Gardeners must have been in demand at the time, for I very soon found a new place at Castlemilk, near Glasgow, and that was the best job I ever had. Kenneth Campbell, the head gardener, who had chosen me, was a kindly and helpful man, and my memory of him is without a flaw.

I lived in the bothy, of course, and my companion there was Ivie Howatson, who was a grand and kindred spirit. But to get to the bothy, I had to brave the trip from the station with Eric Mollison, the horseman, with his trap. Eric was so kindly to his horse that he would not allow the weight of the trap to rest on its back, and the trap had to be balanced very precisely over the wheels. This resulted in a strange seesaw ride, and I don't know of anyone who was not grateful for a lift with Eric from the station, but more grateful that it was only three miles.

Ivie and I cooked our own meals at the bothy, and it was mostly unpredictable, even if sustaining and sometimes mystifying. Oatmeal brose figured largely in our diet, mainly because it was quick and cheap. Another of our favorite and quick evening meals was pancakes. I would mix up a basin of batter — I was good at that, having watched my mother do it so often — and slap spoonfuls of it into the frying pan. With a pound of butter on the table, we would eat the pancakes hot, as they came out of the pan, and grand they were too.

Many years later, when Ivie had risen to the rank of Police Inspector, his first cry when he came to visit would be: 'Come on, Archie, get the brose going!'. It was grand food, and a bowl of it would sustain a man through a day's hard work. A handful of oatmeal, a lump of butter, sugar and salt mixed with almost boiling water, and you were away.

Milk was, for a time, our biggest problem, as Ivie and the cowman, who lived just across the yard, had some kind of bitter quarrel going. The cowman, saying that supplies were short, cut us off from that essential ingredient for our culinary experiments. We were compelled to seek other sources of supply, but certainly had no intention of buying it.

We decided to go for the mother lode, from which, surely, there would be an unlimited supply. In the dark of the night we sallied forth, spurred on by visions of frothing fresh milk. Ivie was hopefully swinging a big jug and I had a bundle of cabbage in my oxter, with which to entice the cows grazing in the field. The first animal was happy to get busy with the cabbage, and Ivie got down on his knees. The flow seemed to take a long time in starting, but he kept at it. He was getting a bit desperate, and his pulling was becoming more energetic; I could feel the cow quivering with each pull, but she must have been a very docile beast. It was no good, and finally Ivie stood up with the still empty jug. 'The bastard's dry,' he said, 'Catch another one.'

The next one seemed to be well nourished and took to my cabbage immediately. Ivie dropped to his knees again and there was a moment's silence as he felt around for the necesary appendage. Suddenly he came alive, the jug was sent flying by a kick from the beast and Ivie was away, running like a startled deer, shouting: 'Christ! it's a bull!' I was right there with Ivie, though, for just as he shouted I had seen the glint of the ring in the bull's nose and was running even before he was, leaving a trail of cabbage.

Our plans for unlimited milk that way had to be abandoned, but there was still hope. That was from the castle kitchen, which in the past had shown signs of being fruitful, if properly cultivated. The cook was a large and kind-hearted woman, a bit past the first flush of her youth, perhaps, but that did not deter Ivie when I told him of the sort of thing that I knew the castle kitchens dealt with. He decided to make the effort, and invited the cook to the pictures. After that it was easy, and our venture paid handsome dividends as the food came rolling in.

We began to grow fat on the handouts from that generous cook, but there was a problem. It seemed that the cook was not only generous but also passionate, and there were nights when Ivie would come in from some session on a cold winter night and complain bitterly, in spite of the bulging parcel under his oxter.   Of course, I had to encourage him, and keep his pecker up as much as possible, for our standard of living depended on it.   'I can't stand much more of this', he would say, and I would point out the joint of roast beef that his session behind the garden wall had produced.   Occasionally, he would jib altogether, and for a couple of weeks or so it would be back to bare essentials for us, until my complaints and his hunger would start another series of nights out and big bundles of food.   It all came to an end, though, when for some reason or another the cook left, and we were back finally to brose and pancakes.

We did get our milk, though, and we got it from the mother lode.   We had both learned now how to manipulate the gear, and our nightly expeditions to the field were routine.   The cowman was puzzled about it all.   His feud with Ivie continued, but somehow we were not short of milk.   Often enough he would try to catch us out, dashing up the bothy stairs when we were at breakfast.   He would rush in, carrying a gift of scones from his wife, who was a first class baker.   We much appreciated those gifts, but were not deceived: we knew them for an excuse.   The express delivery was intended to take us unawares, before we had time for evasive action.   On hearing the clatter of feet on the stairs, the milk jug was immediately off the table and held firm between Ivie's knees, as the puzzled cowman glanced around the bothy, trying to see the source of our supply, and it was obvious that we had some sort of supply, for our bowls of porridge had plenty of milk on them.

Our simple bothy food was certainly sustaining enough, but it did lack variety, especially after we had got accustomed to the gourmet pleasures provided by the acquiescent cook.   After she left, Ivie and I decided that something had to be done, and that it was my turn to do it.   So I turned again to poaching.   Ivie had become friendly with the young gamekeeper, and so we were always pretty sure of where he was each night, and the field was clear enough.   Rabbits, hares and fish were plentiful, and I was soon stocking up our larder again.

The pheasants were easy.   They could simply be driven into the wire fence surrounding the garden. The pigeons were easy, too, but they were legitimate catches, because they were a pest amongst the fruit, and classed as vermin. We used a twelve-bore shot gun to kill them, but it was a noisy thing, and could not be used when I was out after other game. For that, I bought a small gun which was much less noisy. Having bought the gun, I could not afford to buy the cartridges, and so made them myself, loading them with chips of lead which I rolled on an iron plate under a heavy weight. That little gun was very effective at short range, and I filled many a pot with it. There was many a peaceful Saturday afternoon I spent, sitting among the trees and waiting for some victim to come within range.

Once I saw a hare coming along amongst the shrubs. He settled down near me, and I was just taking aim when a stoat appeared in hot pursuit of the hare, who did not seem in the least afraid. The wee beast jumped on the hare's back and scrabbled around amongst the fur at the back of its neck, trying to find the spinal cord, I suppose. It failed there, amongst that thick fur, and so leaped to the ground and ran round to the front of the hare, where he stared up at the face of that huge (to him) animal he was intending to kill, if he could manage it. Both the would-be assassin and myself were having doubts about his ability, and certainly the hare did not seem particularly concerned. The stoat leaped at the hare's throat and tried to sink its fangs in, but quite without success. He spent a bit of time there, but ultimately gave up and dropped back to the ground, flicked his tail and went off in search of something nearer his own size.

Throughout all this, the hare appeared quite unconcerned. It paid no attention whatsoever, but just sat up on its hind legs with ears erect. I was so engrossed by the whole thing that I quite forgot to fire, and the hare just loped away as though the whole episode was an everyday occurence.

Another time, when out alone, I heard what sounded like a rabbit in distress. I followed the sound to the middle of a biggish field, and there, with no other animal in sight was a big buck rabbit, hobbling along semi-crouched, and crying as if in pain. It did not seem to be injured in any way, but just made across the short grass, squealing as though in agony. I soon saw the source of his distress. At the foot of a hedge, about a hundred yards away, I spotted a large stoat, quartering the ground. In a moment he had found what he was seeking — the scent of the rabbit. As soon as he got it, he was moving fast for the rabbit, which had stopped moving and was squatting in the grass, still crying pitiously. I waited until the stoat had the rabbit, then jumped on them both, getting myself an easy rabbit stew. The stoat was certainly not amused by this, and for a moment he stood his ground, chittering in anger, and I thought he might even have a go at me, but finally he fled away across the field. That rabbit could not have seen the stoat, nor could the stoat have seen the rabbit, when I first heard the rabbit's cries, yet each seemed to know the other was there, and knew what the result was going to be.

There were two artificial lakes on the estate, and we were allowed to fish them. They teemed with perch, indeed I believe had been stocked with them for some reason. The perch were spiny and a bit tasteless, but we ate them, as we ate anything we could get hold of. I was sitting on the bank one evening with my rod lying beside me, neither it nor I doing very much, when I was startled to see the rod being slowly drawn into the water. There was a good sized trout on the end of it, and after a bit of bother I grassed it. We found that in fact there were many trout there, but they were bottom feeders, and so had escaped our rods for many a month.

The best catch was made by Hugh, the head gardener's son and myself. The other lake had at some time been used to drive a water wheel, and was fitted with a sluice gate. It was all rusted up and decrepit, but we decided it had possibilities. One summer evening when there was not much activity about the place, and the gamekeeper was well away, Hugh and I took a few tools and a piece of heavy wire mesh down there. After a good bit of fiddling around and a bit of heavy breathing, we eventually managed to get the old sluice gate open and our wire mesh in position. We waited for the fish to come shooting through, and we did not have long to wait. Soon the banks were littered with trout. When the flow stopped, we could see that the mud, which was all that now remained of the pond, was still heaving with fish, and there was nothing for it but to strip and get in there with them. It was a dirty and smelly job, but we finally got all the fish on to the bank, and began to assess the results of our evening's work. We had about a hundred pounds of trout, much more than we could cope with. Fortunately, there were friends in Rutherglen and Cathcart who were more then eager to take them off our hands. They were not very good eating, though, being very old and tasting of mud.

That pond was never filled again, and the identity of the vandals who operated the sluice gate never discovered.

There was one particularly miserable job on that estate, which fell to me, as junior gardener. There was a glen there which was quite literally covered with snowdrops in the spring, and we gardeners spent many hours and weary days picking those miserable flowers and tying them into bunches. The Lady was interested in many charitable causes, and we were all involved at various times in different schemes to make money for them. Selling the snowdrops was one. Selling daffodils was another, in their season.

When there were sufficient bunches, I was detailed to hawk them from a barrow round the streets of Rutherglen. I felt that if the instigator of that scheme had done her share with us, picking them and tying them on a frosty morning down in that glen, she would have lost a lot of her enthusiasm. Anyway, I was equipped with a heavy two-wheeled barrow, probably borrowed from the railway, and turned loose to use my charms to persuade a very reluctant public to '*Buy my pretty flowers*'. If anyone was silly enough to buy a bunch (and they could have got an armful just by taking a stroll through the countryside) I threw in an extra bunch as a bonus. Anything to get that barrow emptied, and get back to my rabbits, trout and pheasants. Indeed, even working was better than selling flowers.

There were quite a number of peculiar animals around on that estate, various cripples and misfits that had been rescued from their fate and were now living in peace and security. One was the heifer with half a tail. The other half had been broken off one night when Ivie and I were indulging in the sport of racing the heifers, with ourselves hanging on to their tails. This particular beast went over a fence. Ivie failed to follow, and was left with half its tail in his hands, while it careered off, even more surprised than Ivie was. Ever after, that half tail stuck straight up in the air was a permanent reminder to us of our misdeeds. The heifer did not seem to mind too much, and certainly thrived.

Perhaps the strangest being around the estate was the laird himself. The Stirling Stuarts of Castlemilk claimed to be of royal blood, and Helen, the daughter maintained that if she had had her rights, she would have been Queen of Scotland. Six feet tall and of regal bearing, she would have been a most worthy queen in any country. And her father would also have made an outstanding and formidable Monarch, at least in appearance.

He always dressed in a very flamboyant mannner, in the most outrageous tweed checks. From his breast pocket there always flew, like some battle standard, a brilliant large red handkerchief, which seemed to be anchored by one corner only. His eccentricities and dress were treated as a joke by the employees, but certainly not to his face, for he had a great regard for his own dignity and demanded the respect he thought due to his position.

He complained one day to the Head Gardener that one of the old men employed in raking up the leaves had simply gone on with his work when the laird passed, instead of stopping to salute. The old man was duly reprimanded, and the next day the laird was treated to an exhibition of how to salute. With cap removed, the old man stood to attention with his rake held rigid in the 'Present Arms' position, quivering with strain, as all good soldiers did. The laird gasped a little, went on, and instructed the Head Gardener to tell the old man not to be a bloody fool. There was no more saluting from the old

man, and no more demands for it: both recognised kindred person-
alities.

'Old Billy', the laird, was certainly the more eccentric of the
two. Each morning he emerged from the front door of his castle and
stood for a moment, sniffing the air. He then moved forward to the
middle of the large gravelled turning area, fumbling with his trousers
as he went. He was a unique man, and insisted on unique trousers.
They had no fly front, but rather a large drop flap secured by two
buttons on the waistband, a very old-fashioned design, never seen
even in those days. With this flap dangling around his knees, the
laird would proceed to relieve himself there in the middle of the gravel,
quite unperturbed by whoever might be watching his performance
with interest, whether they be staff or guests. It was a masterly
performance by any standards, and seemed to embody his attitude of:
'I'm monarch of all I survey, and to Hell with the rest!'.

For more protracted operations, the laird had his own toilet, at the
back side of the castle. There was a grand view of the loch and the
glen from there, and he sat at his ease each morning, surveying his
domain through the open door, again not caring in the least who might
be working about or passing by.

By this time, I had begun to realise that there was not much security
in being a gardener on an estate. Also, I had a met a lassie. This
happened on one of my regular Saturday night visits to Glasgow,
where, in the tradition of all those who had come from the Highlands
and Islands, I spent a good deal of time under the 'Heilanman's
Umbrella'. That was where all the railway lines crossed the street
on a bridge near the Central Station. It was a cold and windy place,
but it was dry, and you could be sure of meeting someone you knew,
and who could talk about the things of home, and who could talk,
moreover, in the Gaelic. Yes, we were grown up and living away
from the islands, but there was no doubt where the heart still
lay. Although it was in truth the Heilanman's Umbrella, others also
gathered there, especially the Doonhamers. Those were the folks
from Dumfries, and they got their name, which is still used, because

157

they always had the same answer when asked where they were going to spend their holiday. It was always: 'A'm gen doon hame.' The lass and I were soon serious, and we still are all these years later, for we married.

I took a course in car mechanics and driving, and to my great surprise, for I had never shown any other academic ability, came out top. So I went off to Camus Esken, at Helensburgh, as a foreman, and was responsible for both cars and gardens. It was a good job, and paid well for the time. I wanted the money badly, for marriage was in the air, but it took me three years to save enough to venture forth on that sea.

Camus Esken turned out to be a poachers' paradise, and I was at it, exploiting it to the full. The owner was a very wealthy man, and reared a lot of pheasants for the pleasure of having his guests shoot them down. There were three gamekeepers employed to look after those pheasants, but I was still able to get my share, and more.

There were two of us in the bothy, Matt and myself, and we often enough cycled off to Glasgow for the evening, arriving back at midnight, tired, and ready for the three or four pheasants which were quietly simmering away on the range. We were very satisfied young men as we swept up the bones and retired to sleep the sleep of innocence. It was really four-star living, and not your usual bothy fare.

It was usually the weekends that provided our best fortune. Most of the staff were away then, and the whole place was a poacher's paradise. There were big pheasant drives occasionally, and then the pickings were really good. All the staff were recruited as beaters, and it was every man for himself. The shot birds were supposed to be picked up, or at least marked and collected later when the section had been shot out. They were marked alright, many of them, but not picked up until the sportsmen were away enjoying their pre-dinner drinks, and it was into the pocket with them. When we came on a wounded bird, we stood on its neck until it stopped fluttering, and noted that one, too.

Prior to one big shoot, it was decided that there were too few birds for the sportsmen, so an urgent message was sent off to a rearer in England to send up a hundred grown pheasants immediately. These were released about the coverts two days before the shoot, but it was found that they had no idea of freedom, nor of what their wings were for. They refused to rise at all as the beaters approached, but just lay cowering in the grass. What a shame! We beaters could not stand on every one of them for later collection, and it was necessary to throw them into the air, shoo them off and tell them to be careful.

A lot of pheasants were reared on the estate, and some of them got into the gardens. That was a bad mistake. A quick dash into their midst would always produce a fluttering handful and a full pot of pheasant stew in the bothy.

I once watched a fine cock bird clean shot in a field where there was a big ash tree. No-one could find that bird when the shoot was over, although all the gamekeepers had seen it fall from the sky. Eventually they gave up, and I was able to retrieve him from where he was hanging in the tree, with his head neatly notched in a forked branch.

Outside the pheasant season, there were always pigeons. We had one particular way of dealing with them which always produced a fine young bird. We climbed the trees where they were nesting just about the time the youngsters were ready to leave the nest. Then we tied the young birds to the branch with a piece of string, and they continued to be fed with 'pigeons milk' by their parents, who were no doubt puzzled why these large youngsters refused to take off into the wide world. They were plump and tender when we went for them, and certainly bridged the pheasant gap.

Well, I stayed at Camus Esken for three happy years, and then married my Doonhamer. We needed a new place then, and went to Troon, but I couldn't settle there. There was too little open country, and too few opportunities for my poaching delight.

So we went off to Bannachra, on Loch Lomond. That was more like it! We were well out in the country, and I was able to provide my new wife with the sort of provisions I had grown to expect over so many years of wandering the fields and woods at midnight. Now, though, I did not have to cook them myself, but I have to say that in those days I knew much more about such things than my Doonhamer did.

To some extent, my poaching at Bannachra was a vendetta against the gamekeeper, with whom I had started off on good terms. My wife's Persian cat disappeared, and she was very upset, and indeed so was I. She had reared it from a kitten, and was very fond of it.

When a cat disappeared in the country, at least in those days, your first thought was of the gamekeeper, for to them anything at all which might in any way threaten their precious pheasants was an enemy. I taxed Willie, the gamekeeper about it, but he denied everything, saying that he was also upset about its disappearance, and that he was himself fond of the animal. Indeed, he might have been, for it had sat on his knee for many an hour by our fireside.

I was not satisfied, though, and spent two days wandering the woods with a spade and a rake, and eventually I found my wife's pet, dead, and pushed down a rabbit hole and covered with soil. When I confronted Willie with the evidence, he said that someone else must have done it. He was guilty in my mind, though, and I warned him there and then that I would destroy his pheasants. That was a terrible threat to any gamekeeper, of course, for his reputation and indeed his livelihood depended on getting as many pheasants as possible in front of the guns.

I went to work with a .410 gun, a handy little thing, easy to carry and conceal, and not too noisy. Of course, I could not buy such a weapon, but it was easy enough to borrow one.

Pheasants are not wild birds at all, and are incredibly stupid. They are specially reared for the shoots, and released into the woods and hedges, where they make their presence known far and wide. Perhaps they are complaining about their sudden change of circumstance from an indolent and well-fed life in the rearing cages to the hazards of freedom. Certainly they have none of the wiliness of native birds like the grouse and partridge, which are not nearly so easy for the poacher — or the sportsman.

Anyway, pheasants always announce their roosting places well in advance of going to their beds. They hang about, cackling and almost crowing before flying up to their roosts. It was no problem to scout around in the gloaming and listen for their announcements. Later, when everyone who had no nefarious business at hand was long in bed, I went out, equipped with gun, torch and bag.

There was no point in going out on a clear frosty night, because then the inevitable rustling and crackling as one approached their roosts gave warning, and they would take off into the clear sky. No, there was no point about '*My delight on a shiny night*' and whoever wrote that song was certainly no poacher. A good poacher had to know his ground so well that he had no need of a shiny night. The ideal is a dark and stormy night, so that when the torch is shone up into the trees where the pheasants are roosting, the birds would be dazzled, but would be having all their work cut out to retain their hold on the swaying branches of the storm-tossed trees.

Once I arrived on the scene, their troubles were over. With the torch held along the barrel of the gun, they were easy to hit, and the roar of the wind drowned the little noise that the gun made. For seven years I continued my vendetta against Willie the gamekeeper, and although he knew perfectly well what was happening, he never once came within an ace of catching me.

I also used gin traps, but they were unsatisfactory, not so much for me as for the pheasants. I found one trap with a pheasant's leg in it, the bird having torn it off in its struggles. That ended that particular technique, so I tried again, with a couple of beans laid on the trap's trigger, and the trap concealed amongst leaves, with only the two beans showing.

It was a nice tempting bite for a pheasant, but the result was devastating, and I never again used gin traps. During the afternoon I was walking round the rose garden with my employer and we were passing the place where my trap was set. Suddenly there was the most alarming noise from behind the bushes, quite horrible screeches of some creature in great distress and pain. The lady exclaimed 'What on earth is that, Cameron?' and I had to invent something about it probably being squirrels fighting. When she ambled off, and it was none too soon for me, I got back to my trap and found, instead of the pheasant I was hoping for, only half a pheasant's head, with the beak still gripping the bean which had been its downfall. I searched carefully, but could not find the sorely stricken bird. It still had its legs and wings, and had gone off somewhere, to die a slow and miserable death. That put me off the pheasants for quite a while, and I gave up my vendetta against the gamekeeper. At least for the time being.

It was tempting, though, especially when the pheasants began to come into the garden, which was my responsibility. I thought of a painless way to reduce their numbers. The wire fences round the garden made an acute angle at one point, and it was easy enough to convert this into a wire cage by fitting a mesh lid where the fences joined. All it needed then was for a few birds to be in the garden when I came out in the quiet mornings. A little judicious herding and hand waving and they were shepherded to the cage. A quick sprint and they were caught, once as many as five handsome cocks. They did not last long then, and that evening my wife and I would be off somewhere on the motor bike I had acquired, with a cloth bag over her shoulder, to visit friends and enjoy a good pheasant stew.

That old motor bike took us many a mile over Scotland, from Fort William to Galloway, and we often enough set out on a journey of a hundred miles or so on icy and snowbound roads. We always got there, too.

One of our favourite outings on a fine summer Sunday was to the top of the 'Rest and be Thankful' Pass. That was a fearsome climb in those earlier days of motoring, although today it has been eased and straightened and simplified. It was really quite an achievement for any car to get to the top, and while we sat and ate our sandwiches or chewed at a few pheasant legs, we enjoyed the spectacle of cars belching steam as they tried to achieve the summit. Many of them

162

would abandon the struggle half way up, the passengers would be disgorged and then it was shoulder power until they reached the first turning place and slid quietly back down the hill. Really, very few cars made it to the summit, but that was no discredit, because it was a very difficult climb for even the most powerful vehicle and the hairpin bend near the top made it tricky, even dangerous.

Apart from the pheasants on our own land, deer occcasionally made a foray from the neighbouring estate of Rosdhu. I managed to get two of them with my .410. The lessons I had absorbed in those long ago days in Rhum came in useful then, as I skinned and butchered the beasts, and once again tasted all the pleasures of deer liver and onions, and venison stew.

One deer eluded me, and the nearest I got to him was a glimpse of his white backside as he jumped the fence on the way home in the early morning. I made careful plans for his downfall, though, by setting up a twelve bore trip gun covering the entrance to the orchard. That was a strictly illegal and dangerous contraption, and I scarcely slept that night as I listened for the explosion of the two barrels. I never heard them, and I was out of bed very early, and away to the trap. I half expected to see the cook or the housemaid stretched out on the grass, because they were both in the habit of going to the orchard at night, but not in search of grass, as the stag was. I was both disappointed and yet intensely relieved to find the gun unfired.

It was quite clear what had happened, and the hoofprints showed it. He had walked right up to the trip wire in the grass, and then stood there shuffling for a moment, looking at the grass on which he had hoped to feed. He then turned away, backed off and jumped the fence. In some way he had been warned that it was fatal to take even one more step forward. He got the message that he was unwelcome, and never came back to the orchard. I never again set a trip gun, and was never tempted to.

That really was the end of my poaching days, for I took another job, after seven years of feuding with Willie the gamekeeper, and living well off his pheasants. This time I went to Largs and worked for

Commander and Mrs Kirkwood as chauffeur and gardener. Those kind and considerate people became my friends, and I stayed with them until nineteen thirty nine, when the war intervened. The armed forces did not have much use for an old fellow of thirty-six, although I may say that at that time I was in the very peak of physical condition, able to work hard all day and all night too, and to run any hill in Scotland. But they had no use for me, and I became a War Reserve Constable in Ayrshire. There are many stories I could tell about that, and many stories I could tell about later years, when at the age of fifty, I went out to Rhodesia and worked on farms there with my son. But they must wait. We'll just let that flea stick to the wa'.

So today I am indeed an old man, the only one left to remember the days when Rhum was a thriving community, and a happy one, except for the midges and the factors. The Doonhamer lass and I are still together, and we still occasionally go to the Heilanman's Umbrella on a Saturday night. But now there is no-one left to discuss which pheasants should fall into the old canvas bag next week.

LUATH PRESS LIMITED

LUATH GUIDES TO SCOTLAND

Written by authors who invite you to share their intimate knowledge and love of the areas covered, these guides are not your traditional where-to-stay and what-to-eat books. They are companions in the rucksack or car seat, providing the discening visitor or resident with a blend of fiery opinion and moving description. Here you will find 'that curious pastiche of myths and legend and history that the Scots use to describe their heritage . . . A lively counterpoint to the more standard, detached guidebook . . . intriguing.'
The Washington Post

'Gentlemen,
We have just returned from a six week stay in Scotland. I am convinced that Tom Atkinson is the best guidebook author I have ever read, about any place, any time.'
Edward Taylor, Los Angeles

SOUTH WEST SCOTLAND: Tom Atkinson
ISBN 0 946487 04 9 pbk. £4.95

This descriptive guide to the magical country of Robert Burns covers Kyle, Carrick, Galloway, Dumfries-shire, Kirkcudbrightshire and Wigtownshire. Hills, unknown moors and unspoiled beaches grace a land steeped in history and legend and portrayed with affection and deep delight.
An essential book for the visitor who yearns to feel at home in this land of peace and grandeur.

THE LONELY LANDS: Tom Atkinson
ISBN 0 946487 10 3 pbk. £4.95

A guide to Inveraray, Glencoe, Loch Awe, Loch Lomond, Cowal, the Kyles of Bute and all of central Argyll written with insight, sympathy and loving detail. Once Atkinson has taken you there, these lands can never feel lonely. 'I have sought to make the complex simple, the beautiful accessible and the strange familiar,' he writes, and indeed he brings to the land a knowledge and affection only accessible to someone with intimate knowledge of the area.
A must for travellers and natives who want to delve beneath the surface.

THE EMPTY LANDS: Tom Atkinson
ISBN 0 946487 13 8 pbk. £4.95

The Highlands of Scotland from Ullapool to Bettyhill and Bonar Bridge to John O'Groats are landscapes of myth and legend, 'empty of people, but of nothing else that brings delight to any tired soul,' writes Atkinson. This highly personal guide describes Highland history and landscape with love, compassion and above all sheer magic.
Essential reading for anyone who has dreamed of the Highlands.

ROADS TO THE ISLES: Tom Atkinson
ISBN 0 946487 01 4 pbk £4.95

Ardnamurchan, Morvern, Morar, Moidart and the west coast to Ullapool are included in this guide to the Far West and Far North of Scotland. An unspoiled land of mountains, lochs and silver sands is brought to the walker's toe-tips (and to the reader's fingertips) in this stark, serene and evocative account of town, country and legend.
For any visitor to this Highland wonderland, Queen Victoria's favourite place on earth.

HIGHWAYS AND BYWAYS IN MULL & IONA: Peter Macnab
ISBN 0 946487 16 2 pbk. £4.25

> 'The Isle of Mull is of Isles the fairest,
> Of ocean's gems 'tis the first and rarest.'

So a local poet described it a hundred years ago, and this recently revised guide to Mull and sacred Iona, the most accessible islands of the Inner Hebrides, takes the reader on a delightful tour of these rare ocean gems, travelling with a native whose unparalleled knowledge and deep feeling for the area unlock the byways of the islands in all their natural beauty.

THE SPEYSIDE HOLIDAY GUIDE: Ernest Cross
ISBN 0 946487 27 8 pbk. £4.95

Toothache in Tomintoul? Golf in Garmouth? Whatever your questions, Ernest Cross has the answers in this witty and knowledgeable guide to Speyside, one of Scotland's most popular holiday centres. A must for visitors and residents alike: there are still secrets to be discovered here!

WALK WITH LUATH

MOUNTAIN DAYS & BOTHY NIGHTS: Dave Brown and
Ian Mitchell
ISBN 0 946487 15 4 pbk. £7.50

Acknowledged as a classic of mountain writing still in demand ten years after its first publication, this book takes you into the bothies, howffs and dosses on the Scottish hills. Fishgut Mac, Desperate Dan and Stumpy the Big Yin stalk hill and public house, evading gamekeepers and Royalty with a camaraderie which was the trademark of Scots hillwalking in the early days.
'The fun element comes through ... how innocent the social polemic

seems in our nastier world of today ... the book for the rucksack this year.' - **Hamish Brown, Scottish Mountaineering Club Journal**
'The doings, sayings, incongruities and idiosyncrasies of the denizens of the bothy underworld ... described in an easy philosophical style ... an authentic word picture of this part of the climbing scene in latter-day Scotland, which, like any good picture, will increase in charm over the years.' - **Iain Smart, Scottish Mountaineering Club Journal**
'The ideal book for nostalgic hillwalkers of the 60s, even just the armchair and public house variety ... humorous, entertaining, informative, written by two men with obvious expertise, knowledge and love of their subject.' - **Scots Independent**
'Fifty years have made no difference. Your crowd is the one I used to know ... [This] must be the only complete dossers' guide ever put together.' - Alistair Borthwick, author of the immortal *Always a Little Further.*

THE JOY OF HILLWALKING: Ralph Storer
ISBN 0 946487 28 6 pbk. £ 6.95

Apart, perhaps, from the Joy of Sex, the Joy of Hillwalking brings more pleasure to more people than any other form of human activity.
'Alps, America, Scandinavia, you name it - Storer's been there, so why the hell shouldn't he bring all these various and varied places into his observations ... [He] even admits to losing his virginity after a day on the Aggy Ridge ... Well worth its place alongside Storer's earlier works.' - **TAC**

LUATH WALKING GUIDES

The highly respected and continually updated guides to the Cairngorms.
'Particularly good on local wildlife and how to see it' - **The Countryman**

WALKS IN THE CAIRNGORMS: Ernest Cross
ISBN 0 946487 09 X pbk. £3.95

This selection of walks celebrates the rare birds, animals, plants and geological wonders of a region often believed difficult to penetrate on foot. Nothing is difficult with this guide in your pocket, as Cross gives a choice for every walker, and includes valuable tips on mountain safety and weather advice.
Ideal for walkers of all ages and skiers waiting for snowier skies.

SHORT WALKS IN THE CAIRNGORMS: Ernest Cross
ISBN 0 946487 23 5 pbk. £3.95

Cross wrote this volume after overhearing a walker remark that there were no short walks for lazy ramblers in the Cairngorm region. Here is the answer: rambles through scenic woods with a welcoming pub at the end, birdwatching hints, glacier holes, or for the fit and ambitious, scrambles up hills to admire vistas of glorious scenery. Wildlife in the Cairngorms is unequalled elsewhere in Britain, and here it is brought to the binoculars of any walker who treads quietly and with respect.

BIOGRAPHY

ON THE TRAIL OF ROBERT SERVICE: Wallace Lockhart
ISBN 0 946487 24 3 pbk. £5.95

Known worldwide for his verses 'The Shooting of Dan McGrew' and 'The Cremation of Sam McGee', Service has woven his spell for Boy Scouts and learned professors alike. He chronicled the story of the Klondike Gold Rush, wandered the United States and Canada, Tahiti and Russia to become the bigger-than-life Bard of the Yukon. Whether you love or hate him, you can't ignore this cult figure. The book is a must for those who haven't yet met Robert Service.

'The story of a man who claimed that he wrote verse for those who wouldn't be seen dead reading poetry ... this enthralling biography will delight Service lovers in both the Old World and the New.' - **Scots Independent**

COME DUNGEONS DARK: John Taylor Caldwell
ISBN 0 946487 19 7 pbk. £6.95

Glasgow anarchist Guy Aldred died with 10p in his pocket in 1963 claiming there was better company in Barlinnie Prison than in the Corridors of Power. 'The Red Scourge' is remembered here by one who worked with him and spent 27 years as part of his turbulent household, sparring with Lenin, Sylvia Pankhurst and others as he struggled for freedom for his beloved fellow-man.
'The welcome and long-awaited biography of ... one of this country's most prolific radical propagandists ... Crank or visionary? ... whatever the verdict, the Glasgow anarchist has finally been given a fitting memorial.' - **The Scotsman**

SEVENS STEPS IN THE DARK: Bob Smith
ISBN 0 946487 21 9 pbk. £8.95

'The story of his 45 years working at the faces of seven of Scotland's mines ... full of dignity and humanity ... unrivalled comradeship ... a vivid picture of mining life with all its heartbreaks and laughs.' - **Scottish Miner**
Bob Smith went into the pit when he was fourteen years old to work with his father. They toiled in a low seam, just a few inches high, lying in the coal dust and mud, getting the coal out with pick and shovel. This is his story, but it is also the story of the last forty years of Scottish coalmining. A staunch Trades Unionist, one of those once described as "the enemy within", his life shows that in fact he has been dedicated utterly to the betterment of his fellow human beings.

HUMOUR/HISTORY

REVOLTING SCOTLAND: Jeff Fallow
ISBN 0 946487 25 1 pbk. £5.95

No Heiland Flings, tartan tams and kilty dolls in this witty and cutting cartoon history of bonnie Scotland frae the Ice Age tae Maggie Thatcher.

'An ideal gift for all Scottish teenagers.' - **Scots Independent**

'The quality of the drawing [is] surely inspired by Japanese cartoonist Keiji Nakazawa whose books powerfully encapsulated the horror of Hiroshima ... refreshing to see a strong new medium like this.' - **Chapman**

SOCIAL HISTORY

CROFTING YEARS Francis Thompson
ISBN 0 946487 06 5 pbk. £5.95

Crofting is much more than a way of life. It is a storehouse of cultural, linguistic and moral values which holds together a scattered and struggling rural population. This book fills a blank in the written history of crofting over the last two centuries. Bloody conflicts and gunboat diplomacy, treachery, compassion, music and story: all figure in this mine of information on crofting in the Highlands and Islands of Scotland.

'I would recommend this book to all who are interested in the past, but even more so to those who are interested in the future survival of our way of life and culture' - **Stornoway Gazette**

'A cleverly planned book ... the story told in simple words which compel attention ... [by] a Gaelic speaking Lewisman with specialised knowledge of the crofting community.' - **Books in Scotland**

'The book is a mine of information on many aspects of the past, among them the homes, the food, the music and the medicine of our crofting forebears.' - **John M MacMillan, erstwhile Crofters Commissioner for Lewis and Harris**
'This fascinating book is recommended to anyone who has the interests of our language and culture at heart.' - **Donnie MacLean, Director of an Comunn Gaidhealach, Western Isles**
'Unlike many books on the subject, Crofting Years combines a radical political approach to Scottish crofting experience with a ruthless realism which while recognising the full tragedy and difficulty of his subject never descends to sentimentality or nostalgia' - **Chapman**

MUSIC AND DANCE

HIGHLAND BALLS & VILLAGE HALLS: Wallace Lockhart
ISBN 0 946487 12 X pbk. £6.95

Acknowledged as a classic in Scottish dancing circles throughout the world. Anecdotes, Scottish history, dress and dance steps are all included in this 'delightful little book, full of interest ... both a personal account and an understanding look at the making of traditions.' - **New Zealand Scottish Country Dances Magazine**
'A delightful survey of Scottish dancing and custom. Informative, concise and opinionated, it guides the reader accross the history and geography of country dance and ends by detailing the 12 dances every Scot should know - the most famous being the Eightsome Reel, "the greatest longest, rowdiest, most diabolically executed of all the Scottish country dances" .' **The Herald**
'A pot pourri of every facet of Scottish country dancing. It will bring back memories of petronella turns and poussettes and make you eager to take part in a Broun's reel or a dashing white sergeant!' - **Dundee Courier and Advertiser**
'An excellent an very readable insight into the traditions and

customs of Scottish country dancing. The author takes us on a tour from his own early days jigging in the village hall to the characters and traditions that have made our own brand of dance popular throughout the world.' - **Sunday Post**

POETRY

THE JOLLY BEGGARS OR 'LOVE AND LIBERTY':
Robert Burns
ISBN 0 946487 02 2 hb. £8.00

Forgotten by the Bard himself, the rediscovery of this manuscript caused storms of acclaim at the turn of the 19th century. Yet it is hardly known today. It was set to music to form the only cantata ever written by Burns. **SIR WALTER SCOTT** wrote: 'Laid in the very lowest department of low life, the actors being a set of strolling vagrants ... extravagant glee and outrageous frolic ... not, perhaps, to be paralleled in the English language.' This edition is printed in Burns' own handwriting with an informative introduction by Tom Atkinson.
'The combination of facsimile, lively John Hampson graphics and provocative comment on the text makes for enjoyable reading.' - **The Scotsman**

POEMS TO BE READ ALOUD: selected and introduced by
Tom Atkinson
ISBN 0 946487 00 6 pbk. £3.00

This personal collection of doggerel and verse ranging from the tear-jerking 'Green Eye of the Yellow God' to the rarely-printed bawdy 'Eskimo Nell' has a lively cult following. Much borrowed and rarely returned, this is a book for reading aloud in very good company, preferably after a dram or twa. You are guaranteed a warm welcome if you arrive at a gathering with this little volume in your pocket.
'The essence is the audience.' - **Tom Atkinson**

SELF-SUFFICIENCY

THE FAT OF THE LAND: John Seymour; illustrated by
Sally Seymour
ISBN 0 9518381 0 5 pbk. £5.50

This was the seminal book by the Father of Self-Sufficiency in
Britain. It is very much a how-to guide to the Good Life, filled to
overflowing with advice from one who has done it all, and
succeeded. It is written with the fervour and enthusiasm for which
John Seymour is noted, and could be dangerous for your future: it
would be very easy to decide to do what he and his wife and young
children did and live literally on The Fat of the Land, almost
entirely divorced from the stresses and strains of modern living.
'It is a favourite dream. I want to recommend this book to them all.
It is a practical, down-to-earth account of one family's adventure in
being self-supporting ... I don't know when I read a book that so
gripped the imagination.' - **The Countryman**

Luath Press Limited

committed to publishing well written books worth reading

LUATH PRESS takes its name from Robert Burns, whose little collie Luath (*Gael.*, swift or nimble) tripped up Jean Armour at a wedding and gave him the chance to speak to the woman who was to be his wife and the abiding love of his life. Burns called one of *The Twa Dogs* Luath after Cuchullin's hunting dog in Ossian's *Fingal*. Luath Press grew up in the heart of Burns country, and now resides a few steps up the road from Burns' first lodgings in Edinburgh's Royal Mile.

Luath offers you distinctive writing with a hint of unexpected pleasures.

Luath Press Limited

543/2 Castlehill   Telephone: 0131 225 4326
The Royal Mile   Fax: 0131 225 4324
Edinburgh EH1 2ND   email: gavin.macdougall@brainpool.co.uk

Please let us have your address (plus fax and email if applicable) if you would like us to keep you informed of future Luath publications.

Most UK bookshops either carry our books in stock or can order them for you. To order direct from us, please send a £sterling cheque, postal order, international money order or your credit card details (number, address of cardholder and expiry date) to us at the address below. Please add post and packing as follows: UK - £1.00 per delivery address; Europe airmail £2.00 per delivery address; overseas surface mail - £2.50 per delivery address; overseas airmail - £3.50 for the first book to each delivery address, plus £1.00 for each additional book by airmail to the same address. If your order is a gift, we will happily enclose your card or message at no extra charge.